Trail Guide Handbook
Cuyahoga Valley National Recreation Area
2nd Edition

The first edition of this publication was made possible
through a generous grant from The George Gund
Foundation, Cleveland, Ohio.

Published by the Cuyahoga Valley Trails Council, Inc.

First printing 1991, second printing 1992.
Second edition, completely revised, 1996.
01 00 99 98 97   5 4 3 2 1

Cuyahoga Valley Trails Council, Inc., (CVTC)
is a not-for-profit, all-volunteer organization dedicated
to building and maintaining trails in the Cuyahoga Valley
CVTC was formed in 1985 from the Ad Hoc Trails
Committee of the Cuyahoga Valley National Recreation
Area Citizens Advisory Commission. Purposes of CVTC
include promoting the implementation of the Cuyahoga
Valley National Recreation Area *Trail Plan*, encouraging
stewardship of trails, and promoting preservation and
conservation of natural areas through public education.
CVTC publishes trail brochures and other educational
materials, circulates a quarterly newsletter,
The Cuyahoga Valley Explorer,
and conducts monthly volunteer trail work projects.
For more information, write:
Cuyahoga Valley Trails Council, Inc., 1607 Delia Ave.,
Akron, OH 44320-1617.

ISBN 0-9630416-1-4
Library of Congress Catalog Number: 92-114089

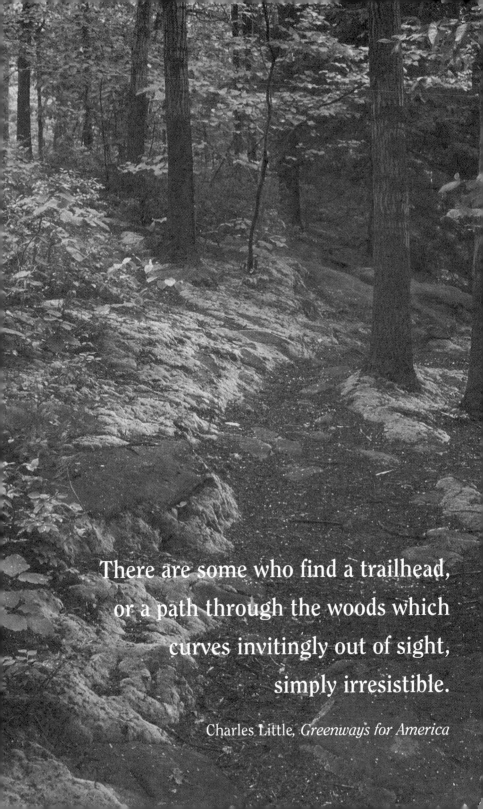

There are some who find a trailhead,
or a path through the woods which
curves invitingly out of sight,
simply irresistible.

Charles Little, *Greenways for America*

Contents

Illustrations

Photographs

Drawings

Historic Photographs courtesy of the archives of Nationl Park Service, Metro Parks, Serving Summit County and Cleveland Metroparks

Map Legend

Main trail	——————
Intersecting, continuing trail	- - - - ——
Trailhead	**P**
Canal (watered/unwatered)	▬▬▬ - - - - -
Picnicking	🛈
Restrooms	🚹🚺
Park Boundary	▬▬▬▬▬
Structure, pavilion, shelter	■
Scenic View	📷

STINKY.
SAND RUN — MINGO TRAIL 3.3 miles
—uphill ⅔rd
GORGE TRAIL / MARK CAMPBELL'S
CAVE & CUYAHOGA — 2.0 miles

[handwritten annotations in top margin: "SOUTH to NORTH", "AMERICA'S HIGHWAY", "HOWARD ST", "MAIN ST", "CUYAHOGA, MEMORIAL,", "MERRYMAN", "RIVERSIDE"]

FORWARD TO THE FIRST EDITION

A Brief History of Trails in the Cuyahoga Valley

The earliest trail builders in our valley were the buffalo (bison) who had a natural knack for the best trail locations including fording places in the streams. The Indians adapted these trails, followed by the early settlers. Many of these trails played an important part in the early history of our nation—as shown on the ancient maps of early North America.

By 1923 when our small band of adventurers sought to "re-explore" the hidden places in the valley, these trails were long ago taken over by the area roadways, or grown over by the natural vegetation. Our small group of art students, garbed in the toughest clothing and shoes available in those popular "Army & Navy" stores of WWI vintage, ventured forth into this tanglewood of dense brush and trees—with barbed wire-like vines and poison ivy—formidable enough to make even Brer Rabbit look twice before entering! Our slogan was from the line in Kipling's poem, "The Explorer," which went something like this: "Something hidden—go and find it—Lost and waiting for you—Go!" and go we did, paying a dear price for the sweat-stained pages in our sketch books!

By the mid-1930s, some trail work was done in the valley, but only within the various parks existing then. This didn't help us much, and we had only the vegetation-choked towpath which ran through the full length of the valley. This trail work was done by the various work relief agencies—the W.P.A. and C.C.C. The latter did much trail work in the Kendall Ledges area.

It wasn't until Cuyahoga Valley National Recreation Area was established that trail work was begun within the valley proper. (How we could have used such trails years ago!) By the year 1991, there were many types of trails within the valley. Ski trails, short trails, long trails, trails to fit all shoe sizes, and even boardwalk trails where needed. Trail building had progressed much from our own early days. They no longer just "grew like Topsy" and ran helter-skelter over the hills and valleys. They are carefully planned now, by park architect and engineer, and carefully built by park crews, aided by groups of volunteer trail builders. (Their combined efforts and results deserve our heartiest thanks!)

The trails described in these pages, remember, are merely "paper trails." "To get the feel and heft of the real trails, you should walk them, savoring each new view along them, ever-changing views, changing from day to day and season to season. Go and find for yourself that "something hidden" which Kipling spoke of!

Joe Jesensky – Akron, Ohio, July 1991

ACKNOWLEDGEMENTS FOR THE FIRST EDITION

Can a committee write a book? After working with the "Big Guide" committee for over a year, we are convinced that this guide could not have been produced any other way! Each volunteer brought to the project his or her unique talent and personal familiarity with the trails of the Cuyahoga Valley. There is no way that all these talents could be found in one person alone. Their unabashed love of the valley and never-failing humor imbued the project with a joy and spirit that kept us persevering through all the deadlines and details.

The project began with an idea, several years ago, about the time that the Cuyahoga Valley Trails Council began producing individual trail guides for Cuyahoga Valley National Recreation Area. Why not print a guide to ALL the trails in the valley? Everyone thought it was a great idea—but who would do it? Then, thanks to the CVNRA staff, we learned that Dave Gates had been thinking about just such a guide. We put out a call for others interested and all of a sudden we had a small— but able— committee to begin what affectionately became known as "The Big Guide". The initial committee included: Peg Bobel, Rob Bobel, Tom Fritsch, Dave Gates, Jack Wenrick, and Jerry Welch.

Next, we needed field scouts to go out, hike or ride the trails, and report back with draft write-ups, and later to return to the field, drafts in hand, to check them for accuracy. We are grateful for the many hours spent hiking the beloved trails of the Cuyahoga Valley (somebody had to do it) by these scouters and writers: Carl Bochmann, Tom Fritsch, Jan Geho, Dick and Yvette Hoffman, Glen and Tom Jenkins, Barb and Mike Kaplan, Kathleen Pettingill, Chuck Urbancic, Annette Wasinski, Vera Riccardi, Dana Smith, Jack Wenrick, Jerry and Cris Welch, Aaron Wester, and Gene Wimmer.

While the scouters were out in the woods, the mappers set about putting lines on paper. Initial drafts were drawn up over a series of hot summer evenings by Rob Bobel, Jerry Welch, and Jack Wenrick , with final maps penned by Rob Bobel and Tom Fritsch. Kim Mueller volunteered to produce the excellent trail-head map. We are grateful to Dave Gates, who did the map photo-reduction and pasteup, and a special thanks goes to Jack Wenrick for generating the wording for the maps, and for acting as courier and making countless runs to keep the mapping moving!

Most of the writing, editing (and typing!) was done by Peg Bobel. Additional writing was prepared by Rob Bobel, Tom Fritsch, Dave Gates, Jan Geho, Jim Sprague, and Donna Studniarz. Rob Muller, who did all the photography, spent many a Sunday looking for that perfect shot that "tells the story". We think you'll agree he did. When we thought who would we most want to write a forward, all agreed that no one would be more appropriate than Joe Jesensky. Thanks also go to our final proofreader, Karen Parsons.

For official review, helpful suggestions, and support of the project, we gratefully thank the staffs of Cuyahoga Valley National Recreation Area, Cleveland Metroparks, and Metro Parks, Serving Summit County.

All this could not be accomplished without funding. We thank Tom Jenkins and the Cuyahoga Valley Association for preparing a funding request, and are most grateful to The George Gund Foundation of Cleveland, Ohio, for awarding us a grant to publish the guide.

The chores of working on this project were always overshadowed by the pleasures of working with the people who made this guide happen. We can not forget to thank the families and friends of the volunteers who assisted or were patient with our obsessions. They were in fact our inspiration.

Rob and Peg Bobel – Akron, Ohio, 1991

PREFACE TO THE SECOND EDTION

When the Cuyahoga Valley Trails Council first published the *Trail Guide Handbook* in 1991, we had to make peace with knowing that trails in the Cuyahoga Valley were changing even as we went to press. Within months of publication the guide was outdated as existing trails were rerouted and new trails were added to the system. Our overzealous consciences envisioned faithful readers standing at some trail intersection scratching their heads and getting frustrated with the discrepancies. Our distress was assuaged when we were reminded that most people have pretty good sense and maybe—just maybe—our little guide wasn't quite as important as we thought. Nonetheless, as soon as we caught our breath from the first edition, we began tracking the changes for this completely revised second edition.

The most significant new trail development in Cuyahoga Valley National Recreation Area (CVNRA) since 1991 is the completion of the Ohio & Erie Canal Towpath Trail. With an impact unlike any other CVNRA trail, the new Towpath Trail defined the recreation area in many peoples' experience. It is the keystone of CVNRA, introducing many new visitors to the park. It stretches the entire length of CVNRA and will soon literally tie the park to the cities of Cleveland and Akron.

Also new since 1991 are the Riding Run, Perkins, and Valley bridle trails. The bridle trails on the east side of the valley now connect to the newest bridle trails on the west side. This totals nearly ten miles of new riding trails. Small portions of the Buckeye Trail have been improved through rerouting, and at the southern end of the park the trail has been moved off the road berm and into a ruggedly beautiful woodland.

Of interest to cross-country skiers, volunteers are constructing the new 4.5 mile Plateau Trail in the Oak Hill Day Use Area. This skiing and hiking trail takes advantage of the extensive wooded area bounded by Riverview, Major, and Oak Hill Roads. Other new trails include Brandywine Gorge (hiking) and Hale Farm (multi-purpose). Mile by mile the park's trail crews, professional and volunteer alike, are completing the recreation area's trail plan. We invite you to seek out and enjoy the new and rediscover the old. You'll walk some trails dating from the 1930s and others as fresh as today.

As this edition goes to press, more new trails and reroutes or extensions of existing trails are on the drawing board. In the next few years look for improvements to the Blue Hen Falls Trail as it leads to Buttermilk Falls and watch for a new Blue Hen Falls trailhead. Also, the National Park Service and the Medina Chapter of the Ohio Horseman's Council have flagged a tentative route to connect the southern bridle trails to the Brecksville and Bedford bridle trails to the north. A little farther out in time are the West Rim, High Meadow, and Five Falls Trails. Both Cleveland Metroparks and Metro Parks, Serving Summit County, are also planning trail additions or improvements.

Those familiar with the first edition of this guide will notice major changes in this second edition. These changes, we hope you will agree, have made the guide more attractive, readable, and easier to use. Again, we have attempted to be as accurate as possible, but must remind you that trail crews and the forces of nature are always at work on the trails, so be aware of possible adjustments in the field!

We are grateful to the following volunteer "revisers" who contributed to this second edition: Dave and Cindy Burgan, Bill Manthey, Kim Norley, Karen Parsons, Jim Sprague, Carolyn Sullivan, and Gene Wimmer. We also thank the staffs of Cleveland Metroparks, Metro Parks, Serving Summit County, and Cuyahoga Valley National Recreation Area, for their review and suggestions. We especially thank our fellow Publications Committee members, Jay Abercrombie, Tom Fritsch, Dave Gates, and Kathleen Pettingill, who contributed hours of labor to making this new edition as up-to-date as possible, page by page and map by map.

Rob and Peg Bobel – Akron, Ohio, November, 1996

Introduction

"Learn of the green world
what can be thy place"
– Ezra Pound

Newcomers to northeast Ohio are often surprised to find a green spot on the map between Akron and Cleveland. The curious discover that green spot to be the Cuyahoga River valley. Exploring the river valley, they are soon forced to give up the "steel mills and cornfields" impression of Ohio. What may come as a surprise to you as well are the cliffs and hemlocks that look like they belong in Canada, the clear, rippling streams coming from forested hills that look like smaller versions of the Appalachians and Alleghenies, and the farmsteads and villages suspended in time.

Much of this green valley is now known as Cuyahoga Valley National Recreation Area (CVNRA), a unit of the National Park System. Of the Cuyahoga River's entire length, one-fourth, or about 22 miles, is within the boundary of Cuyahoga Valley National Recreation Area. The surrounding 33,000 acres of CVNRA are a microcosm of northeast Ohio, both in human and natural history. The national recreation area was created in 1974 through the combined energies of citizens and legislators, all with a strong desire to preserve and protect the green, open space, along with the recreation opportunities and the rich history of the valley. It was created at a time when the National Park Service was seeking to bring parks closer to people and is one of several such urban national recreation areas. CVNRA is now all of northeast Ohio's "back forty" for everyone to enjoy.

CVNRA is a unique park: within its bounds are federally-owned land, privately-owned land, and reservations owned and operated by Cleveland Metroparks and Metro Parks, Serving Summit County, all partners in managing the public areas. In this guide, we describe all the trails within the boundary of the national recreation area, including those managed by the metropolitan park districts. In doing so, we have put in one place information on over 160 miles of trails in the Cuyahoga Valley, hoping to clarify the many choices available to you for hiking, skiing, bicycling, and horseback riding. With guidebook in hand, you can plan your outings, from a short lunch-time walk to an all day trek.

The trail system in CVNRA is actually a "work in progress." In the early 1980s, the founders of the Cuyahoga Valley Trails Council (CVTC) assisted the National Park Service (NPS) at CVNRA in exploring the valley's existing and potential trails. The result of this joint effort was the National Park Service's Trail Plan and Environmental Assessment (1985) for Cuyahoga Valley. Every month CVTC volunteers do a work project to help maintain and improve the existing trails and construct new trails in accordance with the Trail Plan. Of the 115 miles of proposed trails about 55 miles have been completed, some by NPS staff and contractors and some by volunteers, and additional miles are under construction. We will revise this guide periodically as new trails are added to

the system, and we encourage you to be a part of this progress by volunteering
your time and talents to the volunteer work crews.

In this guide, we have described the long distance trails first: the Ohio & Erie
Canal Towpath Trail, the Buckeye Trail, and the Bike & Hike Trail. These are
followed by the rest of the trails, grouped geographically, north to south. For
each trail, you will find a map and description and directions for reaching the
trailheads shown on the trailhead map at the back of this book. The first few
lines of the trail description offer an overview of the trail's general character
and special attributes. The difficulty ratings on the maps are, of course,
subjective, however we have taken into account the distance covered and the
steepness and frequency of climbs—the shorter and flatter the trail, the easier.
In the case of skiing and horseback riding, our ratings assume some beginning
competence in controlling your skis or horse. On the maps we also note
facilities located at the trailheads, using universal park symbols. See the Legend
on page vi for a full listing of symbols. Where there are a number
of trails in one area, we suggest you read the general information on the area
first, then refer to the particular trail you are interested in. Our guide will be
most helpful when used along with CVNRA's free "Official Map and Guide,"
available at CVNRA visitor centers or the more detailed Cuyahoga Valley
National Recreation Area map produced by Steve and Debbie Rhinesmith
of 4 Corners Map Shop in Akron (see Appendix).

Our route descriptions are meant to keep you from getting lost by highlighting
the general route of the trail and making note of intersec-
tions or confusing spots. If the trail is circular, we note in
which direction it is described. Once you are familiar
enough with the trail, try it in the opposite direction.
You'll be surprised how different it looks! This is not
advised on one-way ski trails, however. In those
cases, the trails are laid out in one direction to
make the best use of the terrain and ensure
safety and a sense of solitude on
the trail.

Keep in mind that the soils in this valley, some
of which are loose deposits of glacial material, are
unstable and "flow" when saturated. Flooded
streams can erode banks and deposit trees where
they weren't a day ago. The valley is always
changing, and this means the trails can be
changing too. What we describe today may be
a little different when you go out to hike.

3

We hope that in presenting all these trail options to you, it will help in dispersing use throughout the valley. Some familiar areas can become crowded on beautiful summer weekends, stressing the natural resource and visitors alike. This can be avoided by a little advance planning and seeking the lesser-known areas on busy days. The effects of heavy use in an area are obvious and detract from your experience. You can help minimize your effect on an area by a few simple considerations: please carry out all trash (food refuse left in receptacles at the trailheads tends to get redistributed by scavenging animals), leave the radio at home, control your pets on a leash, and stay on the trail.

In our trail descriptions, we also point out historic features, plants, and animals which you might find along the trail, especially those unique or well-represented in that area. We cannot be all-inclusive, but instead we try to bring your attention to a portion of the rich natural life and cultural history in the valley and hope to whet your appetite for learning more. You will find in your ventures that your pleasure increases as you become more and more aware of the other lives that share this piece of the planet.

THE FOOTSTEPS BEFORE YOU

Before you begin exploring the trails, we would like to tell you some things about this river valley. As you follow the trails of the Cuyahoga Valley, you will be following paths that have seen many other feet before yours. Evidence of human habitation here goes back to about 10,000 B.C., following the last glacial retreat. The glaciers, which had covered the area with ice off and on, 2 to 3 million years ago, ground down and rearranged the hills and drainage patterns. The last glacial retreat exposed a drainage divide, separating the waters that flow to the Gulf of St. Lawrence from those that flow to the Gulf of Mexico. This is the same divide that causes the Cuyahoga River to make a U-turn halfway along its circuitous course from Geauga County to Lake Erie.

Following that last glacial retreat, prehistoric Native Americans hunted mastodons and mammoths. After these early peoples, other native populations emerged, surviving off the rich resources of the river and Lake Erie, and eventually farming and coming together in small villages. Throughout these many years, plant life evolved to the point that the area was covered by a dense, unbroken forest of massive trees. Some of the sycamores along the river were so huge that their hollowed trunks were used for shelter.

The first white explorers, followed by settlers, arrived in this valley in the late

1700s. Following the Revolutionary War, surveying parties made their way to the mouth of the Cuyahoga to begin to measure and map an area known as the Western Reserve. The Western Reserve, stretching 120 miles west of the Pennsylvania border and between the 41st parallel and Lake Erie, was land retained by the state of Connecticut when it surrendered the rest of its land claims to the young federal government. Connecticut then sold the wilderness reserve to the Connecticut Land Company to divide up and sell to eager easterners, both settlers and speculators.

The Cuyahoga River valley was truly "the West," and witnessed a typical phase of pioneering. In 1800, there were 24 million acres of seemingly unlimited forest in Ohio. Seeing these forests as an impediment to raising crops and livestock, the early settlers embarked on an intense cut and burn campaign, not unlike what is happening in South America today. By 1883, the forest cover was reduced to 4 million acres. If you look at canal-era pictures of the valley, you see mostly bare hillsides.

The early settlers could subsist, but could not progress economically, without a means of transporting agricultural products to eastern and southern markets. The canals were a short-lived but successful solution: the first section of the Ohio & Erie Canal was opened in July of 1827, connecting Akron to Cleveland, and by 1840, Ohio led the nation in agricultural production.

The white settlers had other effects upon this land besides transforming forests to farm fields. They quarried stone, then later made use of sand and gravel for concrete building materials. They eradicated predators (at one time there were bears and mountain lions in the valley) and hunted fur-bearing animals, extirpating the beaver. Industries developed and grew, and the towns of Akron and Cleveland began to spread out towards each other.

Beginning around the 1920s, some Ohioans began to value the Cuyahoga Valley in a different way. Seeing an oasis of green between the two industrial cities, they began a conservation movement centered mostly on creating metropolitan park districts. A number of these early conservationists were private citizens who owned large retreats in the valley and wished to see them preserved for public use and enjoyment. Their pioneering preservation efforts led to the establishment of our exemplary metropolitan parks, and eventually to the creation of Cuyahoga Valley National Recreation Area.

THE NATURAL VALLEY TODAY

The deforestation trend that occurred in the Cuyahoga Valley during pioneering times has been reversed, and the valley now supports a diverse wildlife population owing to the variety of habitat types and the many "edges" between forest, field, stream, and wetland. The forests today are second and third-growth, different from the virgin oak, beech-maple, and pine woods. Today we have over 100 species of trees, including red maple, tulip tree, ash, wild black cherry, mixed oaks, hickories, and beeches. Dry uplands are dominated by oaks, while along the river bottoms you find sycamores, willows, cottonwoods, and Ohio buckeyes. The ravines hold relics of the cooler post-glacial period, such as eastern hemlock and yellow birch.

Birds and Beasts

The diversity of habitats in CVNRA makes the area one of the best in the state for birdwatching. Of the 230 or so bird species that have been found in the valley, several especially prefer this area of the state. One is the elusive veery. You may not see it, but are fortunate if you hear its ethereal, flute-like song. The woodcock is another—famous for its spiraling mating display performed in early spring. Turkeys were gone from the valley, but have been reintroduced in the area, and now are seen more and more frequently, though they too are quite secretive.

Your chances of observing other wildlife are quite good, especially if you take some care in your efforts. The best times are early mornings or evenings around dusk. For the best advantage, be quiet, go slowly, and even better, sit still. You won't see wolf or elk, but you could see a beaver working on its dam or a fox or coyote stalking prey. White tailed deer are plentiful. Raccoons, opossums, skunks, and bats are most active at night.

Along with the forests and meadows, your treks will take you through or past wetlands, including streams, floodplains, beaver marshes, and many man-made ponds. These wet habitats are where you can find one of our largest birds, the great blue heron, plus kingfishers, Canada geese, and wood ducks. Several species of native frogs, salamanders, reptiles, and amphibians moving and mating among the cattails and willows are just part of the highly productive wetland world.

Any time of the year, something is happening in the valley, but spring sets the fastest pace. In an astoundingly brief time period, from late March to early June, the valley is transformed from its open, sparse, grey, winter look to a dense, lush, emerald garden. In the midst of this transformation is a window of

6

time in which dainty spring wildflowers bloom. It is also about this time that migrating birds pass through the valley, resting and feeding for a while once insects begin to hatch. The co-occurrence of warblers and wildflowers in early May strains the best of naturalists, worn out by gazing up, then down, up, then down.

In summer, animal activity appears to slow down, especially midday. Early morning, before the mist has burned off, and late evening when the insects and tree frogs begin their serenades, are good times for experiencing summer in the valley. Autumn brings the bittersweet excitement of change and cooler weather, along with the animals' preparations for winter. The height of fall color occurs about mid-October, a popular time for taking to the woods again for the sheer beauty of the scenery. Again, you may sight unusual birds in the valley as they migrate south to wintering grounds. More and more visitors are discovering that winter offers its own special rewards to those who venture out. The starkness and silence are a welcome contrast to the fullness of the leafed-out seasons. You can observe animals by following their signs left in the snow, and given enough snow, you can enjoy the exhilaration of gliding over familiar terrain on skis. There are even special field guides to help you identify plants, trees, fungi, birds, and animal tracks during the winter months.

Rock-hard Facts

For those of you who love rocks, the geology in this area tells the valley's history in deep layers of time. Some of that history is buried far beneath the surface in shales formed from muds deposited in shallow seas 375 million years ago. These Devonian Period deposits are exposed in places where the Cuyahoga River has cut through the layers. Above these are Mississippian shales and sandstones, 330 million years old. The sandstones resist erosion, and when softer rock underneath is eroded, the sandstones sheer off to form cliffs such as those along Tinkers Creek. On top of these layers are the shale, sandstone, and conglomerate laid down in the streams and swamps of the Pennsylvanian Period. These form the surface bedrock wherever they are not overlaid by the younger glacial till. Sharon Sandstone and Conglomerate compose the familiar rock ledges of the valley.

After these Pennsylvanian Period deposits there is a long gap in the geologic record in Ohio—a gap of about 225 million years! In the Rocky Mountains, there are layers of rocks created during that time period, but not in Ohio. It is believed that during this time Ohio was undergoing extensive erosion, up until about 2 million years ago when climate changes spawned enormous polar ice caps which spread southward as glaciers.

These frozen masses, 1,000 to 8,000 feet thick, moved across northern Ohio like giant bulldozers, advancing and retreating in several different ice ages, with the most recent entering Ohio about 25,000 years ago. By the end of their final retreat, they had altered the landscape tremendously, in a scale difficult to imagine. Glaciers changed the course of streams and created new hills, called kames, by depositing tons of till (soils and ground rock). The Cuyahoga River today follows a course that is partly ancient, and partly altered by the glaciers. Underneath part of the Cuyahoga Valley, buried by 500 feet of till, sand, and silt, is a much older valley.

Bedrock in Canada is often exposed over large areas, but here it is only seen in knobs or ledges, and is usually buried by glacial deposits brought down from Canada in the ice sheets. Every time you find a boulder in the valley, you are finding a piece of Canada, usually composed of granite or granite gneiss, brought here during the ice age. In fact, the larger the boulder, the farther away it is from its source.

Animals were plentiful along the edge of retreating glaciers, but these animals were quite different from what we see today. Known as megafauna, these included giant mammoths, beavers, mastodons, and saber-toothed tigers. They are now all extinct. The vegetation changed within a few centuries from predominantly needle-bearing trees to the present day broad-leaved trees. A few of the cooler climate plants still remain, usually found in the cooler ravines.

We have mentioned only a few of the many species of plants and animals you may find here and simply highlighted the natural and cultural history. This is meant to get you started on a long and enjoyable period of exploration. To learn more, stop at the visitor centers in CVNRA. There you will find rangers leading guided walks, exhibits on the natural and cultural history of the park, an introductory slide show, a schedule of programs, general information, and book stores with field guides and local history. Canal Visitor Center is located on Canal Road at Hillside Road. Happy Days Visitor Center is located on State Route 303 less than a mile west of State Route 8. Hunt Farm Visitor Information Center, opened seasonally, is located on Bolanz Road between Riverview Road and Akron Peninsula Road. In addition to these, Cleveland Metroparks operates the Brecksville Nature Center, and Metro Parks, Serving Summit County has the Seiberling Naturealm just outside the southern park boundary. (See Appendix for addresses and phone numbers).

The Cuyahoga River valley holds many surprises. There are those who have repeatedly tramped these "fuzzy green hills", to borrow a phrase from Edward Abbey, and on each return find something new and exciting. We invite you to discover your own special places in the Cuyahoga Valley.

BEFORE YOU HEAD OUT

What to Wear, What to Take

Before you go hiking in Cuyahoga Valley National Recreation Area, guidebook in hand, remember "if you don't like Ohio weather, wait a few hours, it will change!" All kidding aside, we forget that weather changes by the hour, not the day, so prepare for these changes before you set out. John Muir was known to set off into the Sierra Nevada Mountains with just some tea and bread, but most of us are far less tolerant of discomforts than he. A few select items in a daypack or fannypack can help ensure a pleasurable day.

First determine the time you will be out—all day or a few hours. The longer you are out the more protection from changing weather you will require, but even short hikes require a few basics to keep you comfortable and safe. There are 14 basic items that provide you with comfort and protection from almost anything on hikes from 5 to 50 miles. These essentials include: lightweight shell top and bottoms (or a poncho in a pinch), gloves, balaclava or hat, spare socks, down vest (or midweight wool shirt), sunglasses, sunscreen, bug repellent, flashlight, lighter, map and compass, one quart water bottle, snacks, and a small personal first-aid kit.

A lightweight shell top and bottom of a waterproof-breathable fabric (such as Gore-Tex) provides the ideal protection for you, doubling for wind and rain protection in one garment. Though the temperature may seem warm, a quick rain shower and no protection leaves you wet and chilled. At this point you are a prime candidate for hypothermia. Remember that the majority of cases of hypothermia occur in temperatures of 30 to 50°F.

If additional warmth is required, slip a down vest or wool shirt under your shell jacket. A little wind goes a long way to chilling you. With a temperature of 40° F. and a wind of 15 MPH, the wind chill factor is 25° F. Gloves and a hat will help keep your extremities warm. A balaclava (a stocking type cap that can be worn as a hat or pulled down over the face and neck for added protection and warmth) will do the duty of a hat and scarf in cold weather and offers more versatility.

Abundant precipitation in this temperate climate creates a phenomenon which you will come to know, and perhaps even tolerate—mud. Mud is prevalent almost any time of the year, especially where the soils do not drain well—in the stream valleys and even on some of the high ground. Take care to wear adequate footwear and carry spare socks. A change of socks half-way through a long hike will help prevent blisters on tender feet and is a good excuse for a rest stop! If your feet do get wet, the change of socks will feel especially welcome. Also, some people find that wearing a thin pair of liner socks under heavier socks helps prevent blisters.

Sunglasses lessen eyestrain and help reduce the cutting effect of winds on your face. Eyestrain can drain your energy reserves quickly. Protection for your skin is also important: sunscreen and insect repellent should be included in your bag.

One quart of water and some high energy snacks (dried fruits, nuts, sandwich) will help keep you going. Choose foods that give quick energy boosts such as items high in carbohydrates and sugars. Many of the trailheads in the Cuyahoga Valley do not have drinking water, and even where there is water, the supplies are shut down in winter, so carrying water is especially important. When hiking, remember that even if you don't feel thirsty, it's a good idea to take frequent drinks to prevent dehydration. Unless you are familiar with the trail, take along a map and compass. A small flashlight may come in handy if lost, for map reading in the dark, or locating trail markers. Your first-aid kit should include items for blister care, for minor cuts and scrapes, and some aspirin. These items take little space but can make a big difference if needed.

There is not a lot of space in a daypack, so choose clothing with minimal bulk. When hiking in warm weather, make sure there is room for clothing you may remove after you start. As long as you are moving you generate more heat, but when you stop to rest or enjoy the view, you may need an extra layer for chill protection. Remember it is better to be prepared than to get caught short.

Trail Etiquette and Safety

Proper trail etiquette promotes good trail safety; the two go hand in hand. Due respect between all trail users is a wise investment and the returns include a pleasant, enjoyable, and safe trail outing.

The most common type of trail where different types of users will meet is a multi-use trail, although most trails do have more than one use. Therefore a review of some of the common-sense points of etiquette is essential.

Multi-use Trails

- Travel in a normal traffic pattern as on a regular roadway.
- Bicyclists should always voice their presence and what they are going to do when approaching a slower moving user, especially when passing from behind (for instance, "passing on your left").

- In winter, cross-country skiers should do the same.

- If possible, get off the trail or as far to the right of the trail as possible when stopping.

Bridle Trails

- Horses are like people. They all react differently in any given situation. Always bear this in mind when using a bridle trail for any purpose other than horseback riding.

- When encountering a horseback rider, stop, step off the trail, and let him pass. Ceasing activity will prevent any sudden noise or movements that may cause the horse to shy. Stay away from the horse unless the rider invites you to approach him. When the horse has passed, continue on your way.

- Horseback riders should voice their presence if not seen when approaching another trail user.

Cross-country Ski Trails

- When hiking, the main point of courtesy that should be practiced on trails designated for cross-country skiing is to avoid walking in the ski tracks. Footprints in the tracks make a more difficult time for the skier. Walk to the side of the trail, out of the tracks.

- Skiers should voice their presence if not seen when approaching another user.

In General

- Be aware of others who will be encountered on the type of trail you are using.

- Be aware that you, your equipment, and animals with you should be under control. Keep dogs on a leash, horses under control, and any equipment in top condition. Avoid excessive or uncontrollable speed on bicycles, horses, and skis.

- Stay only on trails which permit your use.

- When trails approach private property, please respect the landowner's privacy.

- Pack out trash: garbage placed in trailside containers tends to get strewn through the woods by scavenging animals.

With trail use on the rise, recreational enthusiasts will experience increased interaction between all trail users. Good attitudes and actions on the trail are indeed an investment—in safety—in camaraderie—in future enjoyment of the trails.

Longer Hikes

Several opportunities exist to combine sections of various trails in order to make longer loop hikes. The following are a few suggestions:

Combine a part of the Buckeye Trail with a part of the Ohio & Erie Canal Towpath Trail. Two loops can be made this way, both starting at Red Lock Trailhead. Hike north on the Towpath Trail from Red Lock until it meets the Buckeye Trail at Station Road. At this point, follow the Buckeye Trail west, then south, through Brecksville Reservation. When you reach Snowville Road, follow the connector trail back to the Red Lock Trailhead. Round trip distance is about 10 miles.

The second option, leaving from Red Lock, is to walk south on the Towpath Trail until you reach Boston Mills Road. Here you intersect with the Buckeye Trail which follows Boston Mills Road at this point. Follow the Buckeye Trail west, across Riverview Road, and into the woods. Continue on the Buckeye Trail to Snowville Road. At Snowville, follow the connector trail back to Red Lock Trailhead for a total distance of about 8 miles.

A third loop can be made by also starting at Red Lock Trailhead. Follow the Towpath Trail north until you reach Old Carriage Trail. Turn right (east) onto Old Carriage Trail and follow it until you reach the connector trail to the Bike & Hike Trail. Follow the connector to Holzhauer Road, then Holzhauer Road to the Bike & Hike Trail. Turn right (southeast) onto the Bike & Hike, and follow it to and along Brandywine Road. When you reach Stanford Road, turn right (you will pass Brandywine Falls Trailhead), and go about one-half mile until you reach Stanford Trail, intersecting to the left. Follow the Stanford Trail, eventually passing the Stanford AYH Hostel, and cross Stanford Road. The trail ends at the Towpath Trail. Turn right (north) and follow the Towpath Trail back to Red Lock Trailhead. Round trip is about 8 miles.

Several trails may be combined in the Kendall Lake Area to make longer loops. Studying this guide may give you some ideas, but here are a few suggestions: combine Salt Run Trail and the Cross Country Trail for about a 7-mile hike. Combine Ledges Trail with Pine Grove or Forest Point Trail. You can add Haskell Run Trail or Boston Run Trail to this combination for an even longer hike.

Also for the more adventurous, the O.A. Trail provides a full day—6 to 8 hours—of hiking enjoyment. O.A. stands for Order of the Arrow, which is a brotherhood of honored Boy Scout campers. The trail is often used as a training trail for scouts who are preparing for extended backpack trips.

The O.A. Trail (blazed with a brown and yellow sign with an "O" enclosing the letter "A") is 13.1 miles in length. This loop trail passes through lands in the Boy Scouts' Camps Manatoc and Butler, plus lands owned by Metro Parks, Serving Summit County and others owned by the National Park Service. Parts of the trail follow along roads in the Peninsula area. The O.A. Trail is a rugged trail covering both flat and rolling terrain; sturdy hiking boots are a must for this trail.

Because the O.A. Trail crosses Scout property, permission is required to hike it. You can obtain permission and further information on the exact trail route by calling the Boy Scouts of America Akron Area Council office at 330-773-0415. Hikers who complete the entire 13.1 miles may purchase a commemorative multi-colored cloth patch from the scout council office located at 1601 S. Main Street in Akron.

Equestrians have several opportunities for long, all-day rides. The Wetmore Bridle Trail system on the east side of the valley is linked to the Riding Run and Perkins Trails on the west side via the Valley Trail, allowing for a good, long ride. In the north end of the valley, Bedford and Brecksville Reservations both have several miles of bridle trails which are linked by an unmaintained trail along Sagamore Creek. Another trail linking the northern trails with the Wetmore and Riding Run systems is currently being planned.

Other long-distance combinations may also be possible; these are just a few to whet your appetite. Study this guide to find more combinations for all-day hikes or rides. For bicyclists, the Cuyahoga Valley Trails Council publishes two booklets with suggested rides: *Four Bicycle Trips in the Cuyahoga Valley* and *Five Bicycle Trips in the Cuyahoga Valley.* These can be purchased at the national recreation area's visitor centers or by writing to the trails council.

Off-trail Hiking

In the valley you'll find old roads and animal trails that cross or come near the official trails. There are also picturesque ravines that offer their own little rewards, some with delightful waterfalls. The temptation to go off-trail sometimes gets overwhelming—that enticing animal trail that follows down the ridge, that old roadway that goes up the edge of the gully. But, if you decide to follow this whim, there are several things to think about.

The land within the boundaries of Cuyahoga Valley National Recreation Area is owned by many different entities, so be aware of just where you are and who owns the property. Most areas are clearly posted and signed. Metro Parks, Serving Summit County, has a strict policy of staying on official trails. Their annual ranger-led Stream Stomp is an exception to this policy. Elsewhere throughout the valley, be aware that if you leave the trail you may be straying onto private property and must take care to not trespass. If in doubt, ask permission to pass through a particular area. At all times, please remember that you are sharing this wonderful valley with many other creatures who call it home. Move carefully to minimize disturbance to vegetation or to nesting or resting animals. In stressful weather, disturbing an animal could jeopardize its survival.

Also, be careful! There are obstacles in the woods—fallen trees, multi-flora rose briars, poison ivy, stinging nettles, stumps, and holes, to name just a few. Waterfall and stream bed exploring has its own set of hazards including slippery footing. Go prepared: dress to protect yourself against insects and unfriendly plants.

And please, don't get lost. If you leave the trail, go prepared with a map and compass and know how to use them. There are excellent books on learning the use of map and compass, and the North Eastern Ohio Orienteering Club specializes in cross-country map and compass exploring. You can purchase U.S. Geological Survey maps of the valley at the visitor centers. Most of the valley is shown on two maps, the Northfield and Peninsula Quadrangles. Be aware, however, that these do not show the public and private boundaries, so do some research before leaving the trails.

There are several areas in CVNRA that lend themselves well to cross-country exploring, and these make good practice areas for learning to use a map and compass. In the northern part of CVNRA there is an area known as Terra Vista. It sits on a plateau above the corner of Tinkers Creek Road and Canal Road and includes a couple of small fishing ponds and acres of shrubby, open area that was once a gravel pit operation. Further south, in central CVNRA, is the Kendall Hills area, acres of mowed hills, all interconnected, with splendid views across the valley. And in the southern part of the park, on Riverview Road just south of Bolanz Road, is the Indigo Lake area. Indigo is another good fishing pond surrounded by some open fields connecting to the Special Events Site.

The Trails

State Boat #2 at the Wilson's Mill Lock 37

Ohio & Erie Canal Towpath Trail

On a clear, crisp afternoon in October of 1993, for the first time in over 80 years, a mule crossed over the Cuyahoga River in Peninsula just south of Lock 29 of the Ohio & Erie Canal. The mule and his driver were followed by a procession of people, some in period costumes, some in park ranger uniforms, some walking, some riding bicycles. The event marked the official opening of almost 20 miles of the Ohio & Erie Canal Towpath Trail, stretching from Rockside Road in Valley View to just south of Bath Road in Akron. It was a significant event marking the rebirth of a remarkable transportation route. Today this popular trail is the heart of Cuyahoga Valley National Recreation Area. Exploring this trail you will discover some of the best natural, historical, and recreational features the Cuyahoga Valley has to offer.

A Quick Look

As you travel the entire length of the Ohio & Erie Canal Towpath Trail within the boundaries of Cuyahoga Valley National Recreation Area, you will pass by, under, or over the remnants of a full range of canal related structures including sixteen locks, three aqueducts, two feeder canals, two arched stone culverts, and various weirs, sluices, overflows, gates, and other devices used to control water levels. (North of Station Road, where the canal is still watered, these structures are in use today). Your trip will take you past much of the valley's human history such as Pilgerruh, site of the first known non-native settlement in the valley, some of the most historic homes in the region, a canal mill, farm-steads and fields in production since the 1800s, houses where canal tenders and lock keepers and their families lived, and villages that were once larger than Cleveland.

National Park Service sites along the way help interpret the valley's history: Canal Visitor Center—with exhibits, a bookstore, and programs—introduces 12,000 years of human history and development in the Cuyahoga Valley. The Boston Store, Canal Boat Building Exhibit, tells the story of the canal through its boat builders and watermen. The Stephen and Mehitable Frazee House, oldest in the valley, focuses on settlement, building construction, and the vernacular architecture in the region. Hunt Farm Visitor Information Center presents the life of the farming community. Along the Towpath Trail are numerous informational panels, called "waysides," that will help you understand what you see and, in some cases, what you can no longer see.

As you travel along the canal the evolution of transportation in the valley is all around you. You parallel the first transportation route through the valley, the Cuyahoga River, and the one that put the canal out of business, the Valley Railway. The development of bridge engineering in transportation is evident from an 1882 wrought iron structure to the graceful form of a 1931 concrete arch to major interstate highway bridges whisking today's travelers from rim to rim.

The Ohio & Erie Canal Towpath Trail connects a large number of trails, facilities, and other points of interest. Among the many sites and attractions you will be able to reach, via back roads, connector trails or footpaths, are Hale Farm and Village, Brandywine and Boston Mills Ski Resorts, Brandywine Falls, the Special Events Site, Blossom Music Center, Hosteling International's Stanford House, and Hampton Hills and O'Neil Woods Metro Parks. Along the way you might see deer, a coyote, or skunk and possibly even a beaver or turkey. In spring, be observant for ephemeral wildflowers; in summer look for the white and blue splash of dames rocket; fall is the time for the yellow of wingstem and the purples of Joe-Pye weed, ironweed, and asters.

Things to Keep in Mind

Sandstone mileposts found along the trail mark the approximate location of the original mileposts as recorded on earlier survey maps. These mileposts measured miles from the beginning of the canal near the mouth of the Cuyahoga River in Cleveland's industrial "flats". Therefore, "mile 12" is about twelve miles from Cleveland's Flats following the route of the canal. The original mileposts were determined using the less-than-accurate chain and link method. Extensive washouts from the 1913 flood meant rerouting some lengths of the towpath. As a result, the distance between mileposts is not always 5,280 feet.

The Ohio & Erie Canal, which ran 308 miles from Lake Erie at Cleveland to the Ohio River at Portsmouth, had two high points along its length. Canal locks were always numbered starting from the high point increasing in the direction of the flow of the water. Hence, lock numbers, unlike the mile numbers, increase as the canal heads north.

The Ohio & Erie Canal Towpath Trail is a very popular trail, with 1.5 to 2 million visits per year. Less busy times include weekdays, before noon on weekends, and days with less than ideal weather. Remember it is a shared trail used by hikers and bicyclists and by visitors of varying ages and abilities. Some short sections are also open to horse and rider.

A few tips will help make your trip on the Ohio & Erie Canal Towpath Trail safe and enjoyable; all are based on the golden rule of a shared trail: **be courteous.**

- Travel at a safe speed. Adjust your speed to match traffic flow.

- Keep to the right except to pass others.

- Give a clear warning before passing on the left. Bicycles should be equipped with a bell or horn. If your horn or bell is loud, consider speaking to avoid startling others. "Passing on your left" lets others know in advance of your intentions.

- Everyone yields to horses. If you need to pass, make sure the rider knows in advance that you are passing. Be especially cautious, as horses can be startled by sudden movements or sounds.

- Travel single file when passing or being passed.

- Park regulations note that pets should be on a short (6-foot or less) leash.

- Move completely off the trail when stopped. Obstruction of the trail increases the likelihood of accidents.

Back to the Future

When the first edition of the *Trail Guide Handbook* was published, only parts of the Ohio & Erie Canal Towpath Trail were open for use; much of it was under construction. As this edition goes to press, legislation designating the Ohio & Erie Canal National Heritage Corridor has just been signed by the President. A goal of the planners of the new national heritage corridor is to extend the Towpath Trail north into Cleveland and south through Akron, to Barberton, Massillon and into the village of Zoar. Construction has already begun on portions of the trail in Stark County, and planning is well underway for the trail in northern Tuscarawas County. When the trail is completed, you will be able to climb on your bike and ride from Lake Erie to the historic village of Zoar in Tuscarawas County, a trip of almost 100 miles. Along the way you will be able to sample food in the ethnic neighborhoods of south Cleveland, see the glow from working steel mills, and pass by recycled factories housing tomorrow's industries. Historic sites, restored canal relics, small towns and villages dot the route along with numerous restaurants and shops. You will pass a variety of preserved natural areas—forests, wetlands, and streams. Along the way, using connector trails or side roads you will be able to catch a baseball game, visit a rain forest, or explore a museum.

Yesterday we wrote about the Towpath Trail yet to be in a developing national recreation area. Today we write of a national heritage corridor that will extend the influence of CVNRA throughout northeast Ohio without extending its boundaries. See the Appendix to get more information about this enticing project.

Ohio & Erie Canal Towpath Trail
Lock 39 Trailhead to Frazee House Trailhead

This section of the Ohio & Erie Canal Towpath Trail follows part of the only watered section of the canal in the recreation area. Our description begins at the Lock 39 Trailhead located on the south side of Rockside Road just west of Canal Road. At the southern end of this section, there is limited parking at the Frazee House Trailhead on Canal Road. Additional parking can be found at Canal Visitor Center.

Just north of Rockside Road is the boarding site for the Cuyahoga Valley Scenic Railroad, an excursion train running on the historic Valley Railway. The railroad operates a shuttle service for hikers and bicyclists using the towpath. See Appendix for information.

The section of canal you are about to explore is a National Historic Landmark. This designation recognizes the property as being nationally significant, and although there are many structures and areas listed in the National Register of Historic Places within the park boundaries, this is the only one prominent enough to be listed as a National Historic Landmark.

Your journey begins at Rockside Road in Valley View, near canal mile marker 11. Nearby, the Cuyahoga River makes its way north to Cleveland. Soon the noise of traffic from Rockside Road recedes as you travel south back into a quieter, simpler time. Lock 39, also known as 11-Mile Lock, is just a quarter mile down the trail. Here you find the remains of a small metal bridge at the north end of the lock. This bridge was used by canalers to cross from one side of the lock to the other when the lower gates were open. Less than a mile farther on a road bridge crosses the canal on your left. Stone Road was so named as it was the road used to haul stone from the quarry nearby down to the canal for shipment. Across Canal Road is the majestic form of the Abraham Ulyatt House built in 1849 (private). This house is built of stone in the Greek Revival style and is one of the few such structures remaining in the Cuyahoga Valley.

Just south of Stone Road and to the east is thought to be the site of Pilgerruh, or Pilgrims Rest, where Moravian missionaries and their Christianized Indian followers built the first non-native settlement in the Cuyahoga valley in 1786. Although a historical marker erected further south places Pilgerruh near Tinkers Creek, the fields to your right are believed by most archaeologists to be the actual site of Pilgerruh. A wayside exhibit here tells the tale.

Follow the trail south. Just past Mile 12 the restored 1853 canal-era building located at Lock 38 comes into view. This is Canal Visitor Center, operated by the National Park Service. You may want to stop in and enjoy the canal exhibits

20

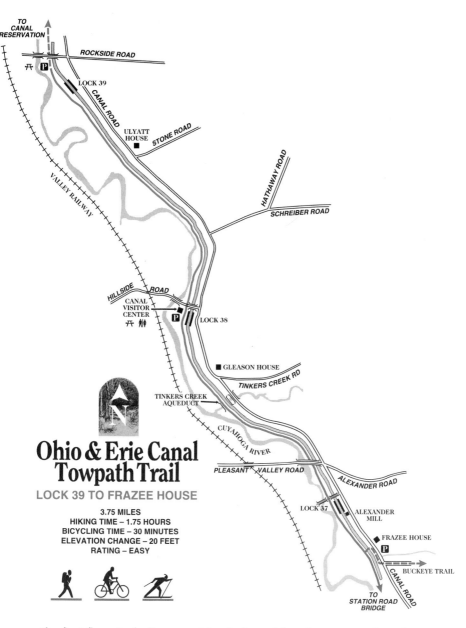

TO
CANAL
RESERVATION

ROCKSIDE ROAD

LOCK 39

CANAL ROAD

ULYATT
HOUSE

STONE ROAD

VALLEY RAILWAY

HATHAWAY ROAD

SCHREIBER ROAD

HILLSIDE ROAD

CANAL
VISITOR
CENTER

LOCK 38

GLEASON HOUSE

TINKERS CREEK RD

TINKERS CREEK
AQUEDUCT

CUYAHOGA RIVER

PLEASANT VALLEY ROAD

ALEXANDER ROAD

LOCK 37

ALEXANDER
MILL

FRAZEE HOUSE

BUCKEYE TRAIL

CANAL ROAD

TO
STATION ROAD
BRIDGE

Ohio & Erie Canal
Towpath Trail

LOCK 39 TO FRAZEE HOUSE

3.75 MILES
HIKING TIME – 1.75 HOURS
BICYCLING TIME – 30 MINUTES
ELEVATION CHANGE – 20 FEET
RATING – EASY

on the first floor, including a working lock model, or learn more about human history of the valley from the excellent exhibits on the second floor. Picnic tables and restrooms are available here.

Take a moment to look over Lock 38 before resuming your journey. In front of you is something that may seem quite simple, but was the evolution of many centuries of trial and error. Coming from Europe, this lock type, known as the two gate lock, is a remarkable piece of engineering. Restored in 1992 to its 1905 condition, Lock 38 is the only operating lock in CVNRA. On summer and fall weekends costumed park rangers and volunteers demonstrate how the power of gravity was used to gently raise (or lower) a fully loaded canal boat eight feet in the lock. You can imagine a canal boat locking through on its way upstream or down. But, the trail beckons us on.

Just a few minutes south of the visitor center is Tinkers Creek Road. The bridge across the canal opposite Tinkers Creek Road once carried traffic from Riverview Road, but the bridge across the river was removed by the county engineer. The canal bridge was closed to vehicular traffic but is still used today by hikers and fishermen. Just beyond, the canal and towpath cross

Lock 38

over Tinkers Creek on the Tinkers Creek Aqueduct. This aqueduct, or bridge of water, is the way canal engineers carried the canal over larger creeks or rivers. It is one of only 14 that were originally used on the 308-mile stretch of canal between Cleveland and Portsmouth, four of which were located on the 38-mile Cleveland to Akron portion. Only this one and the smaller Mill Creek Aqueduct (north of the park near Lock 40) are in use today.

To your left, on the hill above the intersection of Canal and Tinkers Creek Roads, stands the historic Edmund Gleason farm, marked by the huge red English style barn with its distinctive gambrel roof. The Greek Revival farmhouse was built in 1854 and features dressed sandstone. The barn was built in 1905 but no doubt replaced an earlier one, as most farmers built their barns first while living in simple cabins. Then, only after the farm began to prosper, would they improve their own dwellings.

22

After a gentle swing to the east (left) the Towpath Trail again swings right and passes under Pleasant Valley/Alexander Road, bringing you to the only remaining mill structure along the watered portion of the canal. Alexander Mill (now Wilson Feed Mill) was constructed in 1855 and used the excess or waste water which bypassed Lock 37 (14-Mile Lock) to power its grinding wheel. The mill used water power up until 1972 to grind grain but switched to electricity since floating debris kept clogging the water power mechanism. Now grinding has ceased altogether at the mill, but it remains a popular place to purchase feed and seed.

Immediately south of 14-Mile Lock is a bridge on the towpath over a water control structure know as a floodgate. The matter of keeping just the right amount of water in the canal was a never-ending battle. Side creeks, leakage,

Canal Visitor Center

animal holes, floods, and droughts all had to be accounted for, and a floodgate was one mechanism to drain excess water from the canal and drain the canal for repairs. This remains true today, as this one is still used to regulate flow.

South of Lock 37, stop a moment to take in the view. The open pasture to your left, above Canal Road, represents what most of the area looked like 150 years ago. With a little imagination, you can erase the power lines in front of you and turn Canal Road into a narrow dirt path. Down a piece and above this path sits the stately red brick Frazee House. Just north of the Frazee House was a "wide-water", a basin used for layovers and transfer of cargo. The utility poles mark the original location of Canal Road. The basin has been filled in and the road relocated.

There is a small parking lot here, located across Canal Road, next to the Frazee House.

Frazee House Trailhead to Station Road Bridge Trailhead

In contrast to the section of trail north of here, this part of the Towpath Trail is out of sight and sound of any roads. Just south of the Frazee House the canal and path swing sharply away from Canal Road and enter a much narrower portion of the Cuyahoga Valley known as the Pinery Narrows. The Towpath Trail continues through the narrows for about 2.5 miles before reaching the next road—State Route 82, crossing the valley high above the trail.

Park at the north end at the Frazee House Trailhead. The Federalist style Frazee house was finished in 1827. It and the Jonathan Hale Homestead are the two oldest brick houses in the valley. Restored and opened to the public in the fall of 1995, the Frazee House is open seasonally and is well worth the visit. The excellent displays tell about the architecture and craftsmanship of the period. A more spacious parking lot is located at Canal Visitor Center, two miles north. Parking at the south end of this stretch of trail is at the Station Road Bridge Trailhead, located on Riverview Road just south of State Route 82.

From the Frazee House, reach the trail by crossing Canal Road. A short bridge takes you across the canal to the trail. Turn left (south) to begin. Here the Buckeye Trail joins the Towpath Trail from the east on the BT's 1200-mile journey around its namesake state. Be aware that portions of this section of the Towpath Trail are also used by equestrians. Should you encounter someone on horseback, be courteous and step to the side to let them pass.

Cross two water control structures and follow the canal in a gentle curve to the west (right). Here you enter a section of the Towpath Trail that will carry you away from the sounds of internal combustion engines. The Pinery Narrows, or simply the Narrows, is a secluded part of the recreation area protected by the close-in valley walls, wide enough only for the canal, the river, and the Valley Railway.

Just before Mile 15 the trail swings sharply to the east (left). This is Horseshoe Bend, or the Devil's Elbow, so called for obvious reasons. The next two miles in the Narrows are good for spotting wildlife. In mid-summer look for turtles sunning on logs; during a spring evening you might spot a great blue heron silently returning to its roost; winter's snow captures tracks for later observation. Try traveling quietly to see what you can find.

Soon the graceful arches of the State Route 82 bridge, carrying traffic 145 feet above the Cuyahoga River, come into view. This is one of the few remaining bridges which uses parabolic arches of reinforced concrete. Stop for a moment and look around. To your immediate right is the Cuyahoga River—300 years ago

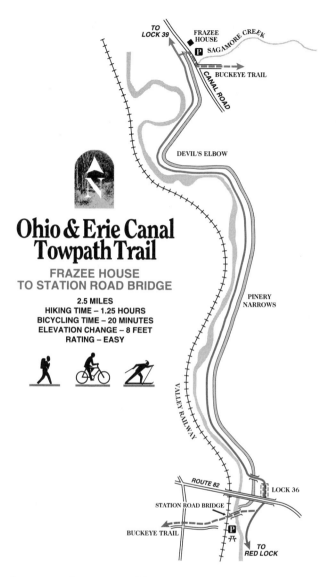

Ohio & Erie Canal Towpath Trail

FRAZEE HOUSE TO STATION ROAD BRIDGE

2.5 MILES
HIKING TIME – 1.25 HOURS
BICYCLING TIME – 20 MINUTES
ELEVATION CHANGE – 8 FEET
RATING – EASY

you may have seen the river used by a group of Delawares transporting furs. To your left is the canal—150 years ago, standing where you are, you may have had to move to let a team of mules pass. Beyond the river is the Valley Railway—120 years back it would have been carrying goods and people up and down the valley faster than the canal. Ahead the Station Road Bridge crosses the Cuyahoga—80 years ago you would have seen it carry one of the first cars across the river. Today, you hear and see traffic on State Route 82 above. Where else can you stand in one location and see over 300 years of the history of transportation?

Just north of the high-level bridge is Lock 36, or 17-Mile Lock (buried during the construction of the bridge). Seventeen-mile lock is also the location of the Brecksville feeder canal and dam, one of three original feeder systems in the Akron to Cleveland stretch of canal. The footbridge here is actually spanning the feeder canal. The main trunk canal is not watered from this point south. Follow the feeder canal to the river to see how the canal gets its water. To reach the trailhead, turn west (right) on the remains of the old Station Road and cross the Station Road Bridge, restored by the National Park Service for pedestrian and equestrian traffic in 1992 and reopened in June of that year. The parking lot is just beyond the bridge. Here the Buckeye Trail leaves the Towpath Trail and enters the splendid Brecksville Reservation. Those looking for longer, more challenging loop hikes should consider combining the Buckeye and Towpath Trails in the areas south of Station Road Bridge.

Picnicking at 17 Mile Lock on The Cuyahoga River – c. 1907

Station Road Bridge Trailhead to Red Lock Trailhead

South of Pinery Narrows, the scenery along the Ohio & Erie Canal Towpath Trail changes compared to that in the Narrows. The canal is not watered here as it is to the north, although small sections of canal intermittently retain shallow water from the many side creeks draining off the hills to the east. The towpath, formerly used as a road in this section, now is lined with trees on both sides, which in some places create an arched canopy to shade the trail. This portion of Towpath Trail serves as access to the Old Carriage Trail, a 3.25-mile cross-country skiing and hiking trail.

Park for this section of Towpath Trail at the Station Road Bridge Trailhead located off Riverview Road, just south of State Route 82. At the south end, park at Red Lock Trailhead on Highland Road (named Vaughn Road on the west side of the river).

S tarting from the Station Road Bridge Trailhead, head towards the bridge. The road takes its name from a railroad depot once located here west of the tracks. The iron bridge, originally erected in 1881 (the date of 1882 on the plaque probably marks the dedication), was restored by the National Park

Ohio & Erie Canal Towpath Trail

STATION ROAD BRIDGE TO RED LOCK

2.5 MILES
HIKING TIME – 1.25 HOURS
BICYCLING TIME – 20 MINUTES
ELEVATION CHANGE – 20 FEET
RATING – EASY

Service and reopened for trail use only in 1992. Note the wooden pavers used as flooring of the bridge, a practice not uncommon at the time the bridge was originally built. Cross the bridge over the Cuyahoga River and continue on the old Station Road until you reach the intersection of the Towpath Trail. Turn right to go south.

Travel is easy and from the trail you can soon again see the river as it slows and enters the slackwater created by the feeder dam downstream of the Station Road Bridge. Soon the river and canal part company as you head towards Lock 35. Also called Kettlewell Lock, after the local canal resident, this lock also gained another nickname, Whiskey Lock, from a still that was located nearby.

Northwest of the lock is a wide meadow-like area lying slightly below the level of the trail. A mining operation removed topsoil from here before the area became a national recreation area. The river flooded the lowered land creating a large marshy habitat. It is slowly filling in and changing into wet meadow, though a small open pond remains and attracts waterfowl.

Cuyahoga River from Route 82 Bridge

Past Mile 18 the Towpath Trail crosses Hooker's Run on a bridge built on the concrete remains of a flood gate dating from sometime between 1905 and 1909. Here, the northern connection of Old Carriage Trail takes off to the east (foot traffic only, PLEASE). Ahead lies a section of Towpath Trail which is, in the estimation of some, one of the most beautiful stretches of the trail in the valley. Away from cars and commotion, this remote trail provides hikers, bicyclists, and skiers a chance to experience a piece of solitude and watch natural habitats quietly reassert themselves after being displaced by the canal.

Just north of Mile 19, you cross a wooden bridge built on the concrete remains of a water control structure called Goose Pond Weir, probably after the name given to a nearby pond. Immediately after the weir is the intersection with the southern connector of the Old Carriage Trail. This connector is paved and open to bicycles and connects the Ohio & Erie Canal Towpath Trail with the Bike & Hike Trail. A small contemporary wooden bridge takes the connector across the canal prism (the name given to the depression which formed the canal).

Soon your trip on this section ends as traffic on Highland Road brings you back to the present century. Just ahead are the remains of Lock 34, also known as Red Lock. The reason for this name is not entirely clear. Although the lock gates were one time painted red, many gates were so painted, so why was this lock called "Red Lock"? The condition of the remaining masonry is a testament to the early use of concrete as a repair material. From 1905 to 1909, extensive

repairs were made on the Cleveland to Akron flight of locks by removing deteriorated stone and replacing it with a concrete facing. Eighty years of weathering have shown their effect.

The parking lot is reached by following a short trail to the left. The small concrete bridge that you cross carries you over the remains of the spillway that directed water around Red Lock.

Red Lock Trailhead to Boston Store Trailhead

After the canal ceased operation, this stretch of Towpath Trail was used as a road by farmers and mill workers up until the 1970s. Now again limited to muscle-powered users, the area boasts a rich habitat of fields, meadows, and marshes. It is here also that, just south of Red Lock, on April 18, 1990, the first spade of earth was turned marking the start of the restoration of the Ohio & Erie Canal towpath as a multi-use trail.

Two trailhead parking lots serve this section of the Towpath Trail. On the north is Red Lock Trailhead on Highland Road and on the south is Boston Store Trailhead on Boston Mills Road. Both are well marked and easy to find.

The trail leaving the end of the Red Lock Trailhead parking lot takes you immediately past Lock 34 (Red Lock) and onto the Towpath Trail. A turn to the right leads north and to the Old Carriage Trail. This description begins with a left turn, south, toward Highland Road. Immediately after crossing the road, look through the trees to your left. The small concrete structures just on the other side of the remains of the canal prism mark the beginning of the spillway for Lock 34. The spillway was a side channel used to carry excess water around the locks. Just beyond, the Towpath Trail swings to the right slightly and joins the entrance road to the site of the former Jaite Mill. At this location, Brandywine Creek slips almost unnoticed under the trail. If you take a moment to scramble down the bank to the east, you will see the graceful, arched stonework of the Brandywine culvert.

The Jaite Paper Mill was built in 1906 and used the plentiful supply of well water in the paper making process. The mill was one of the earliest and largest industries in the valley. The company town just west of here, built to house its workers and company officers, is now used as park headquarters.
The next mile or so of trail carries you past beaver marshes and abandoned farm fields to Lock 33 (Wallace Lock). One-half mile later is the short connector to the Stanford Trail and Trailhead, and the Stanford House AYH-Hostel, run by the Northeast Ohio Council of Hosteling International. This is an excellent and attractive facility for groups, families, or individuals who wish to extend their stay in the valley overnight at a very moderate cost (see Appendix). A one and a half mile hike on the Stanford Trail will yield the 65-foot high Brandywine Falls as a scenic reward.

Continue south on the towpath and find another flooded area. Sharp eyes will be able to spot signs of the beavers' activities. A small wooden bridge over Lock 32 (Boston Lock) provides a good vantage point to watch for wildlife or to view the inside of the lock, known as the chamber. On the east side of the prism you find the remnants of the concrete structure marking the spillway. Ahead and across Boston Mills Road is the Boston Store. Originally built in 1836, it served the canal in a variety of ways and has been restored as a museum of canal boat building, an activity for which the village of Boston was well known. The parking lot and public restrooms are behind the Boston Store.

Ohio & Erie Canal
Towpath Trail
RED LOCK TO BOSTON STORE

1.75 MILES
HIKING TIME – 50 MINUTES
BICYCLING TIME – 15 MINUTES
ELEVATION CHANGE – 15 FEET
RATING – EASY

Boston Store Trailhead to Lock 29 Trailhead

Between the two canal towns of Boston and Peninsula, the Ohio & Erie Canal Towpath Trail snakes its way alongside the Cuyahoga River. Two parking areas serve this section: Boston Store Trailhead off Boston Mills Road at the north end, and Lock 29 Trailhead, in Peninsula on Mill Street, one block north of State Route 303.

If the Boston Store is open, a visit is certainly in order, particularly if your interests include either canal history or boats. The exhibits will give you the true flavor of the art of canal boat building. You can even measure your skill as a craftsman using the many hands-on exhibits. The porch is also a perfect place to meet friends or just reconnoiter before heading out.

As you leave the parking lot, turn south (right) onto a beautiful and well used section of the Towpath Trail. After passing over a foot bridge, a trail to the left leads to an overflow parking lot. You will soon notice that, unlike the canal north of this point, there is no longer a canal prism to your left. Construction of the two sets of highway bridges (I-271 and the Ohio Turnpike) and erosion by the Cuyahoga River have obliterated about one-half mile of former canal bed here. Between the two highways, the Buckeye Trail, which rejoined the towpath in Boston, heads off to the east (left). Just after you pass under the turnpike bridges, the canal prism reappears as a ribbon of wetland on your left, only to be lost again as the trail drops down onto a long, winding boardwalk through Stumpy Basin.

Canalers probably called the area Stumpy Basin from the many stumps of trees removed when the basin was originally built. Such basins were used for boat layovers during the active seasons and boat storage during the winter. The towpath, which in many places was the only barrier between the river and the canal, was breached here in the great flood of 1913. The basin is now an active wetland as seasonal flood waters enter the area. The interpretive wayside on the boardwalk tells how ice was cut from the canal in winter.

Leaving Stumpy Basin, you pass Lock 31, or Lonesome Lock, and just before Mile 23, pass through a tunnel under the Valley Railway. At Lock 30 are the remains of another feeder complex like the one still in use north of Station Road Bridge Trailhead. Although none of the river dam remains, with a little imagination (and help from the wayside exhibit) you can piece together the remaining ruins to see how water was diverted from the river into the canal.

Ohio & Erie Canal Towpath Trail

BOSTON STORE TO LOCK 29

2.5 MILES
HIKING TIME – 1.25 HOURS
BICYCLING TIME – 20 MINUTES
ELEVATION CHANGE – 30 FEET
RATING – EASY

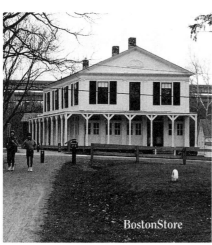

BostonStore

This segment ends in the village of Peninsula at Lock 29 Trailhead. Don't miss the opportunity to explore the chamber of this lock before ending or continuing your journey. Lock 29 is unique because in 1882 it was completely rebuilt with new masonry. This meant the masonry was in good condition during the 1905-1907 repairs when all the other locks had their deteriorated sandstone replaced with concrete. Therefore Lock 29 is the only lock in the Cleveland to Akron section still made entirely of sandstone. Inside the lock chamber, the wayside tells how masons' marks were used to measure productivity and determine how much the masonry crews were paid.

Restrooms and water are available at the trailhead. In the village you can find food, phones, and bike rentals. Peninsula is also a delightful place to explore as it is filled with many historic buildings and a number of arts and crafts shops.

Lock 29 Trailhead to Hunt Farm Trailhead

The section of the Ohio & Erie Canal Towpath Trail from Peninsula to Everett travels through the Deep Lock Quarry area and is used by the Buckeye Trail as it continues its 1200-mile loop of Ohio. The Towpath Trail heads south out of Peninsula and is, as in the northern sections, generally level and easy to follow. Parking for the trail in Peninsula is at the Lock 29 Trailhead located on Mill Street, one block north of State Route 303, north of the downtown businesses. At the south end, park at the Hunt Farm Trailhead on Bolanz Road. The Hunt Farm Visitor Information Center, just across the road from the trailhead, is open seasonally for park visitors.

One hundred and fifty years ago, canal travelers between Cleveland and Akron—moving at a steady three miles per hour—found Peninsula a perfect place to break the journey. It is no wonder that hotels, bars, and other "recreation establishments" soon flourished. It is hard now to imagine that this little village, an island of history not far from modern developments and superhighways, was once the major hub of canal activity for miles around. A walk around town may pique your curiosity further. A visit to the Peninsula Library and Historical Society (on Riverview Road just south of State Route 303) will reveal much of the area's history.

Heading south from the parking lot you will immediately pass Lock 29 and then cross the Cuyahoga River on a pedestrian bridge. This is the location of the Peninsula Aqueduct, one of four original aqueducts used on the Cleveland-Akron section of canal. (The bridge's shape, by the way, was chosen in respect to the curved profile used on one of the other aqueducts, the one over Furnace Run.) Standing in the middle of the bridge looking downstream, you can still make out the trough of the aqueduct by the shape of the massive stone abutments on either side of the river. Looking upstream you will see that the river makes a rather unnatural turn after passing over the remains of a mill dam. This is the result of a rerouting that occurred in the 1880s when the railroad was built. This rerouting cut off a large bend in the river which formed a "peninsula" for which the village of Peninsula was named.

Pass under the State Route 303 bridge. To your right (west) and above you stands the historic Fox House (c. 1880). Faithfully restored by the National Park Service in 1985, this slate-roofed structure stands near the site of one of the Peninsula boat yards. The Fox House now serves as administrative offices for the Cuyahoga Valley Scenic Railroad. Here again the Buckeye Trail joins from the west.

Ohio & Erie Canal Towpath Trail

LOCK 29 TO HUNT FARM

3 MILES
HIKING TIME – 1.5 HOURS
BICYCLING TIME – 25 MINUTES
ELEVATION CHANGE – 25 FEET
RATING – EASY

TO BOSTON STORE

LOCK 29

ROUTE 303

VILLAGE OF PENINSULA

DEEP LOCK QUARRY

MAJOR ROAD
LOCK 28

RIVERVIEW ROAD

CUYAHOGA RIVER

VALLEY RAILWAY

LOCK 27

BUCKEYE TRAIL

EVERETT ROAD

FURNACE RUN

HUNT FARM

VALLEY TRAIL

BOLANZ ROAD

TO IRA

Along this section you notice the distinct shape of the canal bed (or prism) to the west (right), whereas north of Peninsula it is to the east. This is because in Peninsula the canal itself crosses the river, and the towpath must always be located between the canal and the river. The switch from west to east occurs just north of Lock 29 at exactly the same place the present day trail crossed the lock. The towpath was always located between the canal and the river, serving two purposes. First, it acted as a dike to keep the canal out of the river and the river out of the canal, and second, this location kept it away from the hillside and the potential of being washed out by side creeks.

Soon the trail takes you into the Deep Lock Quarry area. A small footbridge to the west marks the northernmost extent of Deep Lock Quarry's Towpath Trail. Just over half a mile from Peninsula, you find the magnificently preserved remains of Lock 28, or Deep Lock. At 17 feet, this lock had the largest drop of all the locks on the 308-mile long Ohio & Erie Canal. The usual drop on a lift lock was 8 to 12 feet. The additional depth apparently was not economical and the canal builders never repeated the experiment.

You may want to spend a moment at this lock (remember to move off the trail when stopping). Note the holes in the top of the lock wall. These are locations of wooden mooring posts used to tie the boats to the sides to prevent them from bumping about in the lock chamber during filling and draining. Other features not visible in watered locks can be seen, such as the square openings in the lock walls used as culverts to move water from high to low level when the gates were closed.

Back on the trail, cross under the Valley Railway and head south. The scenery here is a pleasant mix of farm fields, river, and floodplain. In winter you notice your proximity to Riverview Road, which parallels on the west (right), but summer's foliage hides all but the occasional sound of a car or bicyclist passing by. In this stretch of trail the agrarian setting in the valley is preserved. The rich bottom lands of the Cuyahoga River have been farmed for thousands of years, and the National Park Service has developed a leasing program to keep these fields farmed. Without it, these fields would slowly go into succession, losing an important page of the cultural history of settlement and development of the valley.

Just north of Mile 27 stands, coincidentally, Lock 27 (Johnnycake Lock). This marks your arrival at the community of Everett. Here the canal crossed Furnace Run, for which Furnace Run Metro Park, far upstream, is named. A wayside at the lock tells how the lock got its nickname. From the pedestrian bridge over Furnace Run you can see the remains of the stone abutments of the Furnace Run Aqueduct. In low water, you can see small iron pins built into the stone used to tie the iron work of the aqueduct to its supports. Just before the bridge, the Buckeye Trail leaves again heading west toward Hale Farm and Village.

The little hamlet of Everett developed in the canal days, grew to a population of 150, and in the early 1970s still had a small population and supported a gas station and general store. Everett was included in Cuyahoga Valley National Recreation Area when the park was created in 1974, and the National Park Service subsequently purchased many of the structures. Things were quiet in the hamlet until 1993 when the park service began the process of restoring the structures, two or three each year. Most of the buildings have been converted into residential facilities for the teaching staff working at the Cuyahoga Valley Environmental Education Center on Oak Hill Road. The remaining buildings are used as offices, library, and storage for historic documents and artifacts. Everett's church is thriving and the hamlet is slowly coming back to life.

Your trip ends at the Hunt Farm Visitor Information Center, a restored late 19th century farm complex. Opened seasonally, it has a small display and sales area. Here you will find restrooms, water, and a public phone.

Hunt Farm
Visitor Information Center

Stopping for a rest

Hunt Farm Trailhead to Ira Road Trailhead

Parking is available at both ends of this length of trail. The Hunt Farm Trailhead is on Bolanz Road, which runs between Riverview Road and Akron-Peninsula Road. The Hunt Farm Visitor Information Center is across the road from the trailhead. South, parking can be found at the Ira Trailhead, off Riverview Road just north of Ira Road.

Before beginning your trip south, take a moment to visit the Hunt Farm Visitor Information Center (open seasonally). Hunt Farm is typical of the many small family farms that were throughout the valley at the turn of the century. This is a good opportunity to pick up a park map or fill your water bottle, as this is the southernmost towpath facility with public water.

From the parking lot, turn south (left) onto the trail and immediately cross the remains of a stone floodgate historically used to drain excess water from the canal. In a short distance you will pass behind a small trailer park. Just south of the trailer park is a bicycle connector trail to Hale Farm and Village. This mile-long trail will take you past a boarding stop for the Cuyahoga Valley Scenic Railroad, alongside spring-fed Indigo Lake, then over a wooded ridge above Hale Farm, with an exceptional view into the pastoral setting below. If your time permits, a visit to Hale Farm and Village (Western Reserve Historical Society's reconstructed 19th century farmstead and village) is definitely worthwhile.

Continuing south on the Towpath Trail, you will enter an area of canal that is, most of the year, rich in wildlife. For the next three-quarters of a mile or so, you will travel along a portion of canal rewatered by nature's own engineer, the beaver. This large member of the rodent family has been in residence in this vicinity for almost twenty years, since just after the formation of the recreation area. If you are observant, you will see not only beaver-chewed stumps and mud-and-stick dams, but also lodges and possibly tracks and drag marks where the beavers have hauled tree limbs.

Here also the trail passes a bend in the Cuyahoga River, another good spot to observe geese, ducks, and other water-loving birds. A wayside tells of the river's role as a pre-canal transportation route and how it failed the need of early settlers, leading to the building of the canal.

Just past Mile 28 you will enter the heart of the beaver marsh. The National Park Service built the boardwalk here, slightly to the east of the location of the original towpath, to minimize impact on the rich habitat of the extensive wetlands. This is an excellent place to observe wildlife, so much so that the Ohio Department of Natural Resources has selected the marsh boardwalk as an official "watchable wildlife" viewing site. Benches and an observation platform were built into the boardwalk to provide places for observation or contemplation.

Next, beyond the end of the boardwalk, you reach Lock 26, or Pancake Lock, whose nickname came from a tale not unlike the one attributed to Lock 27's nickname of Johnnycake Lock. In both cases, a flood caused the canal to be temporarily impassable, and as the story goes, the travelers were fed meals made from the freight on board—cornmeal. The Ira Trailhead parking lot is found a short distance past Lock 26.

TO LOCK 29

HUNT FARM

BOLANZ ROAD

VALLEY TRAIL

RIVERVIEW ROAD

HALE FARM TRAIL

CUYAHOGA RIVER

INDIGO LAKE

BEAVER MARSH

SPECIAL EVENTS SITE

VALLEY RAILWAY

LOCK 26

IRA

IRA ROAD

TO INDIAN MOUND

Ohio & Erie Canal Towpath Trail

HUNT FARM TO IRA

1.75 MILES
HIKING TIME – 50 MINUTES
BICYCLING TIME – 15 MINUTES
ELEVATION CHANGE – 6 FEET
RATING – EASY

Ira Road Trailhead to Indian Mound Trailhead

This section of the Towpath Trail is unique in that the canal and towpath south of Ira Road were destroyed by the construction of the present day Riverview Road. The trail here was built entirely west of the canal and only comes close to the location of the original towpath at two places, where the trail explores the remains of the two locks found in this section.

Parking at the north end is at Ira Trailhead, off Riverview Road just north of Ira Road. The south end of the trail is serviced by Indian Mound Trailhead, the largest trailhead in the southern end of the park. It is also on Riverview Road, about one-quarter mile south of Bath Road.

Follow the short trail east out of the parking lot at Ira Trailhead to the Towpath Trail. Note the wetland created by the remains of the canal prism. The trail to the left (north) will take you to a boardwalk over a beaver-created marsh. It is a unique place to observe wildlife, particularly at sunrise or sunset, so unique in fact that the Ohio Department of Natural Resources has selected the beaver marsh boardwalk as an official "watchable wildlife" viewing site. Once on the towpath, turn right (south) and follow the trail to Riverview Road. The trail crosses Riverview and Ira Roads to continue on the west side of Riverview Road. Remember to use caution, especially with children, when crossing at this busy intersection.

Here, near the intersection of Riverview and Ira Roads, was a crossroads known as Ira. Ira was first called Hawkins, named after a local resident, until it became a mail stop on the Valley Railway. But the mail got mixed up because of a town called Haskins in another part of the state so the railroad changed it to Mr. Hawkins' first name, Ira.

The trail along here is bordered by a pleasant mix of hardwoods in the lowlands and has a few slight changes in elevation not found on the other portions of the Towpath Trail. The east walls of both Locks 25 and 24 were demolished and the canal prism filled in when Riverview Road was widened in the 1930s. Between the lock remnants a drive leads up to the historic Botzum farmstead.

Here you also parallel the Valley Railway. Built in the 1880s, the railroad carried passengers until 1963 and freight until the mid-1970s, hauling coal to Cleveland from southern Ohio and West Virginia and iron ore south from Cleveland's harbor. In 1987 CSX (successor to the Baltimore & Ohio) sold the Akron toIndependence stretch of railroad to the National Park Service. A scenic excursion train, which began running on the line in 1975, has been operating on it ever since. (See the Appendix for information on the Cuyahoga Valley Scenic Railroad.)

Just after passing Mile 30, you will cross Bath Road where, once again, the Buckeye Trail joins the towpath and heads south into Akron on its way to Cincinnati. Your journey ends about one-third mile south of Bath Road at Indian Mound Trailhead. The trailhead takes its name from nearby hills thought to be Adena burial mounds.

Ohio & Erie Canal Towpath Trail
IRA TO INDIAN MOUND
1.75 MILES
HIKING TIME – 50 MINUTES
BICYCLING TIME – 15 MINUTES
ELEVATION CHANGE – 25 FEET
RATING – EASY

On the trail

The Buckeye Trail

When traveling from Cleveland to Cincinnati, most people follow I-71. Less well-known routes comprise the Buckeye Trail, a 1200-mile path marked by blue blazes, which encircles the state of Ohio. Buckeye Trail Association, Inc., the group that supports the Buckeye Trail, is happy that the trail passes through the Cuyahoga Valley. These sections of the Buckeye Trail are among the most scenic in the state.

Within the boundaries of Cuyahoga Valley National Recreation Area, the Buckeye Trail remains mostly off-road from its entry into Bedford Reservation near Egbert Road and Gorge Parkway to the intersection of Everett and Riverview Roads. The trail is along roads through the reconstructed covered bridge on Everett Road and past Hale Farm and Village to permit those using the trail to enjoy these historic spots without straying far from the trail. South of Hale Farm the trail is again in the deep woods of the western rim of the valley, then leaves the national recreation area just south of Bath Road.

Whichever direction you follow the Buckeye Trail in the Cuyahoga Valley, north or south, Cincinnati is less than 600 miles away. Along the way to Cincinnati, the trail travels through both glaciated and unglaciated terrain across Ohio's bluegrass country, its plains, and its hills. The trail traverses abandoned homesteads, strip mines, abandoned railways, towpaths of the historic state canal system, little-used country roads, levees, and even city streets. At present, about a third of the trail is off-road. The Buckeye Trail links to a nationwide system of long distance trails, making it possible to walk by trail from the Cuyahoga Valley to the far corners of the United States.

Throughout the state, the Buckeye Trail is built and maintained entirely by volunteers. Except where the trail follows existing public trails or uses public land, no public assistance has been used to develop or promote the Buckeye Trail. Built primarily for hikers, the trail is open to all users without charge. However, users must determine and obey whatever rules are imposed by the landowner. In some places the blue trail markers may be faded almost beyond recognition. In certain sections, the trail may be overgrown or muddy. However, with some determination, adequate preparation, and trail guides, the hiker will experience great pleasures!

The 34 miles of Buckeye Trail within CVNRA are described in detail in the following pages. The route runs generally north and south, traversing the length of the Cuyahoga Valley from Bedford to Akron. In the heart of Brecksville Reservation is a unique three-way intersection of the Buckeye Trail, where north, south, and west routes meet. This intersection also marks the official site of the formal completion of the trail.

If you are out for a really long hike, or preparing for backpacking, the Buckeye Trail is ideal. In the Cuyahoga Valley you can link portions of the Buckeye Trail with other trails (such as the Ohio & Erie Canal Towpath Trail) or with sections of roads, to make long loop hikes. Suggestions of such loops are in the section "Longer Hikes" in the Introduction.

The Buckeye Trail is marked with blue blazes on trees and posts. At trail junctions, watch for blue blazes to point the way. Where the trail changes direction, the blazes are positioned one offset above the other. The offset of the upper blaze indicates the direction the trail turns. Where the Buckeye Trail goes through land owned by Metro Parks, Serving Summit County and in CVNRA along the Ohio & Erie Canal Towpath Trail, the trail is marked by wooden trail signs.

Buckeye Trail Association, Inc., which maintains this trail, is a non-profit, tax-exempt, all-volunteer Ohio corporation organized and operated exclusively for charitable and educational purposes. The goal of the association is to construct, maintain, and encourage use of the Buckeye Trail. For membership information and guides to the Buckeye Trail in other parts of Ohio, write: Buckeye Trail Association, Inc., P.O. Box 254, Worthington, OH, 43085.

Buckeye Trail

Egbert Picnic Area (Bedford Reservation) to Frazee House Trailhead

The Buckeye Trail from Egbert Road to Alexander Road doubles as a bridle trail in some sections; in these sections it is wide, well-graded, and has a stone surface. From Alexander Road on, it is a narrow footpath. Hemlock ravines, waterfalls, rock ledges, and historic sites all combine to make this a favorite area for hiking or riding. The trail is linear, requiring you to double back or spot a car at the end.

The Buckeye Trail enters the northeast corner of Cuyahoga Valley National

Recreation Area near the intersection of Egbert Road and Gorge Parkway in Bedford Reservation. (See page 71 for more information on Bedford Reservation). The parking nearest to the Buckeye Trail in this east end of the reservation is at the Egbert Picnic Area on Gorge Parkway, just north of Egbert Road. There is additional parking at different points along the trail: Lost Meadows Picnic Area, Bridal Veil Falls, Tinkers Creek Gorge Scenic Overlook, a small lot at the corner of Overlook Lane and Egbert Road, the trailhead parking lot on Alexander Road, and at the Sagamore Grove Picnic Area. Parking at the south end of this section is at the National Park Service's Frazee House Trailhead on Canal Road just west of Sagamore Road. There are restrooms and grills at the picnic areas. A ranger station and public restroom are located at the intersection of Egbert Road and Gorge Parkway.

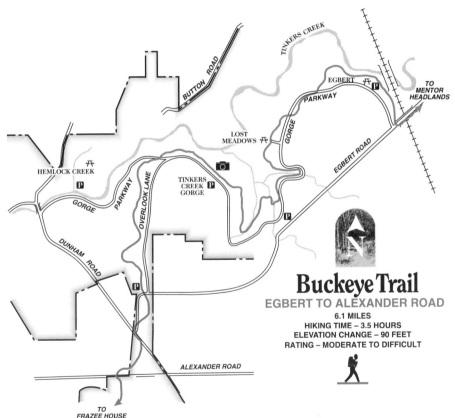

Buckeye Trail

EGBERT TO ALEXANDER ROAD

6.1 MILES
HIKING TIME – 3.5 HOURS
ELEVATION CHANGE – 90 FEET
RATING – MODERATE TO DIFFICULT

The Buckeye Trail is described north to south. Begin this section of Buckeye Trail at the Egbert Picnic Area. The trail runs along the rim of Tinkers Creek Gorge, just behind the picnic shelter. Take the access trail to the right of the restrooms to reach a good view of the gorge. Turn left onto the Buckeye Trail and follow the blue blazes.

For a short distance the narrow trail hugs the edge of the steep gorge and is lined by a wooden fence. Shortly after the fencing ends, make a sharp turn away from the gorge, continuing to follow the blue blazes. A side trip to the right on the Bridle Trail takes you down to Tinkers Creek, its shale cliffs, and the site of the old Powers Mill.

The Buckeye Trail heads south towards Gorge Parkway. Before reaching the parkway, cross the All Purpose Trail and the Parcourse® Fitness Circuit, then cross the parkway to the south side of the road. Wind up and down along Shawnee Hills Golf Course then come back across Gorge Parkway and the All Purpose Trail. About 500 feet beyond this crossing, a foot path leaves the Buckeye Trail, leading down to Lost Meadows Picnic Area. This is an interesting area to explore, with a pretty waterfall among the hemlocks.

Continue on the Buckeye Trail which now combines with the Bridle Trail. The next road crossing is at the drive leading to Lost Meadows Picnic Area. Cross the drive to continue on the trail. Here you enter an area of hemlock ravines with views of Deerlick Creek and its waterfalls to the right. The trail then comes out to the edge of Gorge Parkway, crosses the creek, and follows along the rim of a ravine.

Now about 2 miles from your start, you join the trail coming down from Gorge Parkway leading to the Bridal Veil Falls Overlook. Cross Silver Creek on an arched bridge. The overlook is to your right.

Leaving the overlook, follow the blue blazes on through a mature woods of oaks, hickories, and beeches, for about a mile. At this point you reach the Tinkers Creek Gorge Scenic Overlook that provides views into the 200-foot-deep Tinkers Creek Gorge, a National Natural Landmark.

Past the overlook, the Buckeye Trail, now again separated from the Bridle Trail, continues to the intersection of Gorge Parkway and Overlook Lane. Just west of the intersection, cross the road and rejoin the Bridle Trail. Here the trail bears away from the road and enters a deeply wooded area. The Bridle Trail and Buckeye Trail are combined until the Buckeye Trail takes a sharp turn away from the Bridle Trail to lead you to an old stone quarry. Watch carefully for the blue blazes, following them around the quarry and back to the Bridle Trail. Shortly after this, you come to a grove of pines then reach Egbert Road, now 4.2 miles from your start.

Cross Egbert Road, continuing to share the path with the Bridle Trail as both descend to the end of Egbert Road at Dunham Road. Here the Buckeye Trail turns to the left and uses the All Purpose Trail.

In a very short distance, however, the Buckeye Trail leaves the All

Purpose Trail, crosses Dunham Road, and shortcuts to rejoin the All Purpose Trail at Alexander Road.

Cross Alexander Road; the Cleveland Metroparks Bike Trail parking lot is on your right. Continue south on the Buckeye Trail; here it joins the Bike & Hike Trail, both using an old railroad grade. In less than a third of a mile, watch for the place where the Buckeye Trail leaves the railroad grade to the west (right), descending the embankment. Here the trail changes dramatically: it is again a narrow footpath and follows the very rim of the Sagamore Creek gorge. You can get the clearest views into the wooded creek valley in the wintertime. Two 25-foot waterfalls can be seen from the trail; winter is also their best season, when ice decorates the cascades and neighboring shale cliffs.

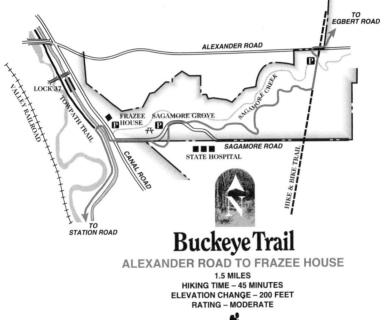

Buckeye Trail
ALEXANDER ROAD TO FRAZEE HOUSE
1.5 MILES
HIKING TIME – 45 MINUTES
ELEVATION CHANGE – 200 FEET
RATING – MODERATE

The narrow gorge of Sagamore Creek widens into a broader valley, with the whitish upper branches of sycamores indicating the floodplain below. Continue on the Buckeye Trail as it comes out to Sagamore Road near the Sagamore Grove Picnic Area (where there are restrooms and a shelter). Leaving the Sagamore Grove Picnic Area, cross the road and follow the blue blazes into the woods (watch carefully for the blazes here), then after a short ways come back out to Sagamore Road and follow it to Canal Road. The Buckeye Trail turns north and follows Canal Road for a short distance. End this section of Buckeye Trail at the Frazee House Trailhead on Canal Road just north of Sagamore Creek.

Frazee House Trailhead to Station Road Bridge Trailhead

This section of the Buckeye Trail has two special attributes: it is almost entirely level and goes through a unique roadless area of the valley known as Pinery Narrows, following the Ohio & Erie Canal Towpath Trail.

To access the north end of this section of Buckeye Trail, park at the Frazee House Trailhead located on Canal Road just north of Sagamore Road. The historic Frazee House, completed in 1827, is one of the oldest brick residences in the county. The National Park Service restored the house and opened it to the public in 1995. The excellent exhibits tell the story of the settlement of the Connecticut Western Reserve and the architecture and craftsmanship of the time.

To begin your hike, cross Canal Road and the canal to reach the trail on the opposite side of the canal. Turn south (left) to continue on the Buckeye Trail. The Buckeye Trail follows the Towpath Trail route to the south for the next 2.5 miles where the canal passes through a very narrow section of the Cuyahoga River valley. You can find a special quiet and remoteness here where the trail, out of sight of any roads, is closely bordered by the Cuyahoga River on one side and the watered canal on the other. The hustle and bustle of canal days is far removed from today's quiet. Also gone are large stands of majestic white pines that gave this area its name, Pinery Narrows. In the 1800s they were cut for masts and floated to Lake Erie for the Great Lakes sailing ships. In the 1880s the Valley Railway's guidebook referred to this area as Little Packsaddle Narrows.

At the southern end of this section you pass under the graceful arches of the State Route 82 bridge.

Pine Hill Road, which becomes Station Road on the other side of the river, intersects with the trail. These roads are no longer used as public roads. To follow the Buckeye Trail, turn to the right (west) and cross the Station Road Bridge. The National Park Service restored the iron bridge in 1992 for pedestrian, bicycle, and horse traffic. The original bridge, constructed in 1881, served as an important vehicular link from east to west across the Cuyahoga River. A stop on the Valley Railway was located on the west side of the tracks not far from the stop used by the Cuyahoga Valley Scenic Railroad today.

The trailhead parking is located just south of the bridge.

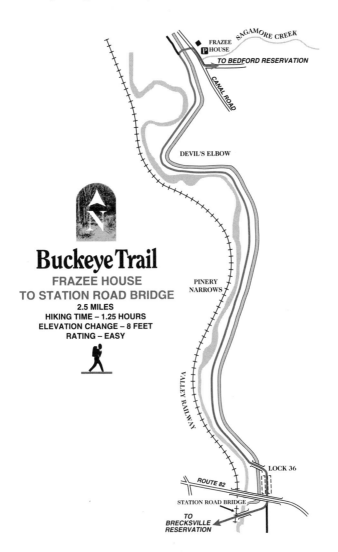

Buckeye Trail
FRAZEE HOUSE
TO STATION ROAD BRIDGE
2.5 MILES
HIKING TIME – 1.25 HOURS
ELEVATION CHANGE – 8 FEET
RATING – EASY

SAGAMORE CREEK

FRAZEE
HOUSE

TO BEDFORD RESERVATION

CANAL ROAD

DEVIL'S ELBOW

PINERY
NARROWS

VALLEY RAILWAY

LOCK 36

ROUTE 82

STATION ROAD BRIDGE

TO
BRECKSVILLE
RESERVATION

Station Road Bridge Trailhead to Jaite (Red Lock Trailhead)

In this section, the Buckeye Trail leaves the river valley, climbs 200 feet towards the west rim of the valley, wanders through much of Cleveland Metroparks' Brecksville Reservation, then traverses up and down several stream ravines before descending once again to the valley floor. It is marked throughout the length by blue blazes painted on the trees.

To reach this section from the north, park at the Station Road Bridge Trailhead located east of Riverview Road just south of State Route 82. The trailhead is located opposite an entrance to Brecksville Reservation. Since this is a linear trail, you need to arrange to leave a car at the other end or return on the same route. Or, if you are in the mood for a long loop hike, you can return via the Ohio & Erie Canal Towpath Trail. Parking at the south end of this section is at Red Lock Trailhead on Highland Road, .5 mile from the Cuyahoga Valley National Recreation Area Headquarters at Vaughn and Riverview Roads. A spur trail connects Red Lock Trailhead to the continuation of the Buckeye Trail. This section, like the other sections of Buckeye Trail in this guide, is described from north to south.

From the parking lot at Station Road Bridge, follow the paved trail that parallels the entrance road, walking towards Riverview Road. Continue across Riverview Road, now on the paved All Purpose Trail and Parcourse Fitness Circuit. Cross Chippewa Creek on a footbridge. Watch for where the Buckeye Trail now crosses Chippewa Creek Drive—the entrance road to the Plateau Picnic Area is across the road. The Buckeye Trail crosses Chippewa Creek Drive and climbs steps to the left of the entrance road, sharing the path with the orange-marked My Mountain Trail. Now once again the Buckeye Trail is a narrow footpath that starts you on an interesting tour of the lesser traveled parts of Brecksville Reservation.

Follow the blue blazes up towards the top of the ridge. At the top of this first climb a spur of My Mountain Trail goes left. Bear right to continue on the Buckeye Trail. Cleveland Metroparks is managing this forest area to encourage wildflowers and the continued health of this oak-hickory forest. Bear right where a side trail comes in from the left. (This side trail, a former route of the Buckeye Trail, leads to Riverview Road.)

Continue southwesterly on the Buckeye Trail. In a short distance My Mountain Trail leaves the Buckeye Trail to return to Plateau Picnic Area. The Buckeye Trail briefly uses the All Purpose Trail, then crosses Valley Parkway (Oak Grove Picnic Area is to your left). Here you are about one mile from the start of your

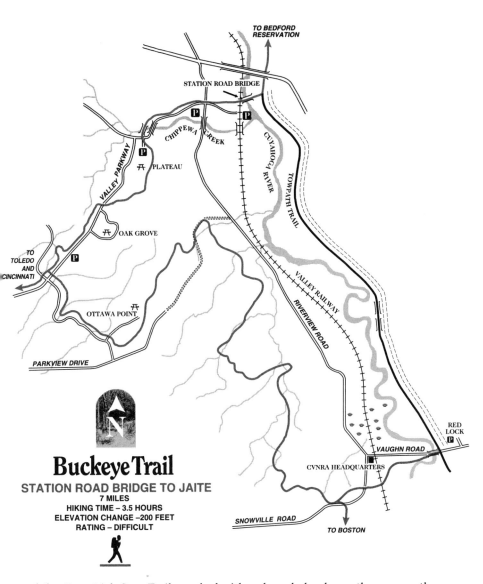

Buckeye Trail

STATION ROAD BRIDGE TO JAITE
7 MILES
HIKING TIME – 3.5 HOURS
ELEVATION CHANGE –200 FEET
RATING – DIFFICULT

hike. Deer Lick Cave Trail, marked with red symbols, shares the same path. A cross-country ski route is also marked on the trees with blue skiing symbols. Now on the north side of the road, follow the trail just below the level of the road, paralleling the road, until you come to the Buckeye Trail signpost. This three-sided signpost shows you where you are in relation to the entire Buckeye Trail. Donated by Cleveland Metroparks, this sign marks the spot where the Buckeye Trail was officially completed, linking all four corners of Ohio. If you continue west, you can reach Cincinnati in 441 miles; continuing south you

51

can reach Cincinnati in 552 miles, and turning back and going north you can enter Headlands Beach State Park after only 65 miles.

At this point, you can take a side trip to explore the Deer Lick Cave area. To do so, follow the western leg of the Buckeye Trail, paralleling Valley Parkway. The Berea sandstone formation is just to the west of the signpost along the trail. Steps lead down into the cave area, rich with fern gardens and plush mosses. Return to the three-sided Buckeye Trail sign to continue south on the Buckeye Trail. (The Buckeye Trail section heading west soon leaves the reservation.)

Leaving the sign, cross Valley Parkway and the All Purpose Trail, following the blue blazes. The Buckeye Trail joins the Bridle Trail just across the road. Continue with this Bridle Trail for .7 mile. At the next major trail junction, the Bridle Trail crosses the road to go to the stables; stay on the Buckeye Trail on the east side of Meadows Drive. It narrows to a footpath again. You can see an abandoned quarry near the trail.

At the entrance to Ottawa Point Picnic Area, the Buckeye Trail joins the entrance road into the picnic area. This is a reservable area; if it is in use, please respect the privacy of the picnickers. Follow the blue blazes into the picnic area, then again pick up the footpath near the parking lot. Now you are traveling east before turning south again.

Beyond the picnic area, take the trail through a mixed pine/hardwoods forest, then descend to cross a creek. After leaving the creek, the Buckeye Trail parallels then goes onto the abandoned section of Parkview Road; watch for the next turn, to the right, when the Buckeye Trail leaves the old road. For the next two miles you travel south again, climbing into and out of several small valleys. The woods vary from young stands of aspens to mature oaks, and lush fern gardens carpet areas along the creeks. Near the end of the two miles of ups and downs, you climb out of the wooded valley to an open, meadowy ridge near Riverview Road. Cleveland Metroparks is managing this area for bluebird habitat. Follow the grassy lane south through the meadows, keeping watch for the beautiful bluebirds.

Watch for the blue blazes which lead you back into the woods and down to a creek. Cross this creek several times, working your way towards Snowville Road. You come out into a meadow with patches of dogbane, milkweed, and wild berries, just before reaching the road. White-tailed deer frequent this area, and if you're lucky you might also catch a glimpse of a red fox or coyote.

At this point you have several options, depending on where you left a car and your time constraints. To go further on the Buckeye Trail, turn left, walk along Snowville Road a short distance, then turn right, cross Snowville Road, and enter the woods on a narrow footpath. The next road crossing is at Columbia Road, 2.2 miles away. If you left a car at Red Lock Trailhead, or wish to return via the Ohio & Erie Canal Towpath Trail, turn to the left and walk along Snowville Road, then cross Riverview Road. Follow the trail through the fields, out to Vaughn Road, then across the river to the trailhead. A round trip can be made by following the Ohio & Erie Canal Towpath Trail back north (considerably flatter, faster, and shorter than your trip south). And of course your other option is to return on the same trail, which will look entirely different traveled in the other direction!

Jaite (Red Lock Trailhead) to Boston Trailhead

The Buckeye Trail in this section continues as a narrow footpath. From the trailhead the trail climbs to the west rim of the Cuyahoga River valley, then following a north-south course it crosses several tributaries which flow into the Cuyahoga River. These side ravines and intervening woodlands are typical of the beautiful forested terrain of the Cuyahoga Valley. Blue Hen Falls, towards the southern end of this section, is a good destination for lunch, additional exploring, or photography. You can return along the same trail, retracing your steps, or use the Ohio & Erie Canal Towpath Trail to make a loop hike of about 8 miles.

This area is rich in local history. The northern trailhead is named after Lock 34 on the Ohio & Erie Canal, found next to the parking lot. Over 100 years ago the area would have been crowded and noisy as farmers brought their products to a loading basin near here to be transported to markets via the canal. In the early 1900s, paper maker Charles Jaite built a mill south of Highland Road along Brandywine Creek. In addition to the mill, he constructed a company town to house workers and the company store. Seven of the ten buildings remain and have been faithfully restored to their original appearances, including their banana yellow color. They now house the National Park Service headquarters for CVNRA. The Buckeye Trail also passes near the North District Ranger Station which is housed in a restored brick home built in the 1800s by Jonas Coonrad, one of the early prominent citizens of Brecksville. In addition to farming, he operated a cheese-making business on his homestead.

For access to this section of the Buckeye Trail, park at the Red Lock Trailhead on Highland Road, .5 mile from park headquarters at the intersection of Riverview and Vaughn Roads (Vaughn Road becomes Highland Road east of the Cuyahoga River). Three-quarters of the way along this section there is a small parking area at Blue Hen Falls on Boston Mills Road, one mile west of Riverview Road. The southern parking lot is the Boston Trailhead, located on the south side of Boston Mills Road just east of the Towpath Trail. There are restrooms and water at the Boston Store, and portable toilets at the other trailheads.

Beginning from Red Lock Trailhead, cross the river, then cross over to the south side of Vaughn Road and go south along the river and through the field. This is a short access trail linking the trailhead with the Buckeye Trail. Follow the trail signs under a powerline, across the Valley Railway, then across Riverview Road. Go about 200 yards up Snowville Road, then turn left, cross the road and enter the woods. Watch for the trail sign marking the turn.

Follow the blue blazes through the woods until you come to a set of steps built into the steep hillside. These steps were built in 1990 and 1991 by volunteers taking part in American Hiking Society Volunteer Vacations. Imagine what the climb was like <u>before</u> the steps! This climb takes you about 140 feet above the valley floor.

At the top of the hill, turn to the right and follow an old farm road along the ridge. Massive oak trees line the trail, with beech trees on the slope off to the right. When the leaves are off the trees there is a good view towards the south. There you can see the handsome, brick Coonrad house and its bright red barn. The house is now the North District Ranger Station.

Just beyond a radio tower and block building, the trail comes out into the open, jogs left, then right. Watch for the blue blazes here when returning as it's easy to miss this jog.

This open area, created by utility corridors, is a couple hundred feet above the valley and is an

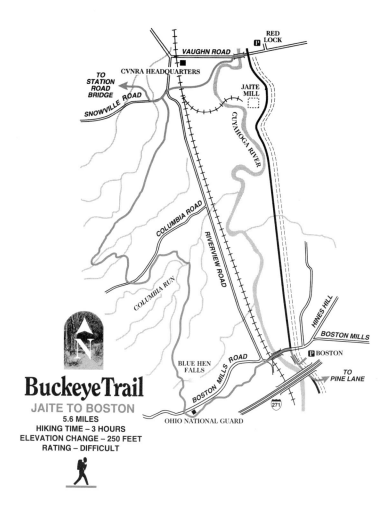

BuckeyeTrail

JAITE TO BOSTON

**5.6 MILES
HIKING TIME – 3 HOURS
ELEVATION CHANGE – 250 FEET
RATING – DIFFICULT**

especially good place for sighting hawks and turkey vultures soaring on thermals. Songbirds prefer the edge along the meadow and forest. It is worth it to have carried binoculars with you at this point. You can observe songbirds close by or enjoy the spectacular, long views.

After crossing the utility right-of-way, continue on an old one lane road through the oaks and maples. Watch for the cutoff to the left, following the blue blazes. Beech trees become more prominent as you cross a small ravine, then a larger ravine, crossing a creek on stepping stones. Steps notched into the slope lead the way up the other side. The trail then widens again through fields and soon reaches Columbia Road.

Cross Columbia Road. The trail now parallels Columbia Road for a short distance, just below the level of the road. A hemlock ravine slopes off to the right. Further along, some foundation stones and large oak trees surrounding a clearing are all that remain of an old homestead.

Soon the trail begins to descend towards the ravine formed by Columbia Run. Thick, green moss and graceful, evergreen hemlocks framing a small clearing above Columbia Run make this an especially attractive spot. Hemlocks can be found in scattered locations throughout the state, but they need a moist, cool environment such as this ravine.

Cross Columbia Run, then watch carefully for blue blazes pointing the way up out of the ravine. At the top, follow the ridge until you reach another utility right-of-way. Just after this right-of-way the trail drops down towards Spring Creek.

A side trail leads to Blue Hen Falls. This falls, like others in the valley, drops over Berea Sandstone to the less resistant Bedford Shale below. By continuing downstream on the Blue Hen Falls Trail you can reach Buttermilk Falls, formed on Bedford Shale. By following streams this way and observing the banks, you can see the layered rock of northern Ohio exposed like layers of a sliced cake.

 Back on the Buckeye Trail, leaving Blue Hen Falls, cross Spring Creek on a wooden bridge, then follow the paved path to a small parking area and cross Boston Mills Road. Here the trail climbs the hill towards I-271. Follow the blue blazes through woods paralleling I-271, into an open field, then through Ohio National Guard property. Past the barracks and caretaker's house, follow the trail down an eroding road and across a creek. After the creek, there is a set of 87 steps to take you back up to the ridge. Follow this ridge, then wind down a steep, and often slippery, hill ending at Riverview Road.

Cross Riverview Road and follow the blazes along Boston Mills Road through Boston, crossing the Cuyahoga River then coming to the Ohio & Erie Canal Towpath Trail at Boston Store. The Buckeye Trail turns onto the Towpath Trail continuing south. The trailhead parking is beyond, on the south side of Boston Mills Road. You can make a long loop hike by returning north on the level Towpath Trail.

Boston Trailhead to Pine Lane Trailhead

This section of the Buckeye Trail is a narrow footpath on the east rim of the Cuyahoga Valley. It takes you through some terrain that has been altered by the construction of major highways, but also goes into less disturbed areas. Because of this, there is a wide variety of habitats along the trail, including old orchards, a borrow pit, mature oak woods, and the pristine Boston Run valley. Through these different areas, you can find an equally diverse collection of plants and animals.

Parking for the Buckeye Trail is at Boston Trailhead on Boston Mills Road, .1 mile east of Riverview Road. At the south end is Pine Lane Trailhead: going east out of Peninsula on State Route 303, watch for the trailhead sign indicating a left turn onto Pine Lane. The trailhead is down the road, on the right.

Starting from Boston Trailhead, find the trail by walking south (towards the I-271 bridges) along a service road. Here you briefly join the much busier Ohio & Erie Canal Towpath Trail. After going under the I-271 bridges, look for a sign directing you uphill and left across a wide field and into the woods. Entering the woods, the trail continues to climb, passing through an oak/hickory forest and an old apple orchard. Further along, you go through a beech/maple woods, then come out into a field along the Ohio Turnpike. Blue blazes on shrubs and trees lead the way away from the highway and back into the woods.

Follow the blazes in and out of grassy and forested areas until you reach Boston Mills Road. Cross the road, turn right and follow Boston Mills Road for about 100 yards, then turn left into the woods, where the trail follows a wooded ravine. Follow the blue blazes along the ravine, then back onto Boston Mills Road. Turn left to cross the bridge over the Ohio Turnpike. At the end of the bridge, turn right to cross the road again and climb the short hill into the woods along the highway.

Here you find a stand of white pines, once plentiful in the Great Lakes region. They are easily identified by long, soft needles in bundles of five (five needles, five letters in w-h-i-t-e). On the whole, Ohio forests are mostly deciduous. Among the conifers, only white pines, eastern hemlocks, and tamaracks are native to this area, and they only grow in specific localities where their habitat needs are met. These pines were undoubtedly planted here, as they are in straight rows.

BuckeyeTrail

BOSTON TO PINE LANE

4 MILES
HIKING TIME – 2 HOURS
ELEVATION CHANGE – 240 FEET
RATING – MODERATE

A whole book could be written on these lovely trees; they, more than any other type of tree, starred in early white settlement of this continent, being used for everything from giant masts of sailing ships to homes, bobsleds, covered bridges, and roof shingles. When this country was first settled by Europeans, huge stands of white pines stretched for miles; an early pioneer saying declared that a squirrel could travel its lifetime without ever coming down from the pines. Our original stands in the valley are all gone. The widespread decimation of the native pines contributed to the start of the conservation movement. Now white and red pines, which are tolerant of low moisture and nutrient levels in soils, are planted in disturbed areas to hasten the restoration of forest cover.

Along the trail and to the right of these pines is a depression that was made when soil was dug for the Ohio Turnpike bridge embankments. This is an interesting area to explore for unusual plants such as the fringed gentian which blooms in the fall. Deer browse this area and in summer you can frequently hear the field sparrows calling from the taller shrubs. Listen for the deliberate opening notes speeding to a trill. Some have likened it to a coin spinning to a stop on a table.

At the end of the pines, turn right (watch carefully for this turn—an old lane goes straight and a bridle trail crosses) and follow the Buckeye Trail through the oak woods along the south side of the depression, then bear left and wind around the head of a side ravine, crossing two small drainages. An almost pure stand of young oaks is growing here on the uplands. Continuing on, a small pond marks a former home site to the right of the trail just before you reach Akron Peninsula Road (closed to vehicles).

Turn to the left, walking east along Akron Peninsula Road, and watch for the blaze and sign marking the point where the trail leaves the road and reenters the woods. This last mile of trail goes into and out of the Boston Run valley. This rich, moist valley is full of ferns and wildflowers: hepatica in delicate shades of pink or blue, trillium, toothwort, violets, and wild geranium are just a few of the flowers that can be discovered here in the spring. You might also hear the flutelike song of the wood thrush or the clear, musical song of the hooded warbler, both elusive birds of northern woodlands.

A log bridge with handrail has been placed across Boston Run for the crossing. After the steep climb out of the creek valley, follow the trail across a utility cut (the openings off the utility cut can be obscured in the dense growth of summer), then through a pine planting, and finally into the parking area at Pine Lane Trailhead.

Pine Lane Trailhead to Everett Road Covered Bridge

Here the Buckeye Trail allows you to leave the hills behind and enjoy an easy walk along the Ohio & Erie Canal Towpath Trail. Along or quite near the trail you can visit two canal towns, two canal locks, and a former stone quarry at Deep Lock. There is enough to explore along the way to warrant allowing plenty of time for this hike, especially if you are interested in canal history.

The Pine Lane Trailhead located off State Route 303, .7 mile east of Peninsula, serves the north end of this section of trail. This segment ends at the restored Everett Road Covered Bridge, a scenic spot for a picnic. You must return along the same route or arrange to leave a car at the end of your hike.

To begin, look for the blue blazes directing you west out of the Pine Lane Trailhead parking lot and onto an old road (Pine Lane). Follow the road until it ends and the trail becomes a narrow path on a brick roadbed. This was an earlier roadbed of State Route 303; you can still find remnants of the old guardrail.

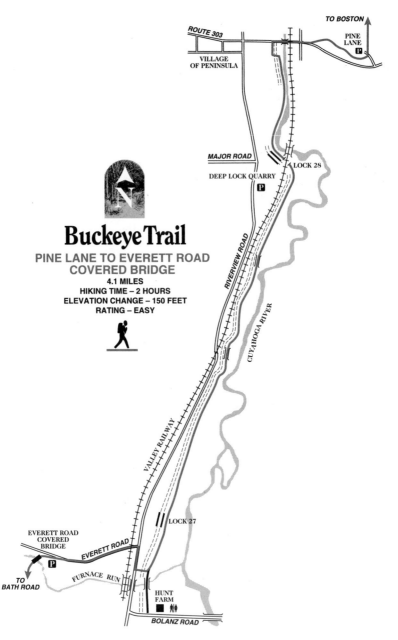

TO BOSTON

ROUTE 303

PINE LANE ℗

VILLAGE
OF PENINSULA

MAJOR ROAD

LOCK 28

DEEP LOCK QUARRY ℗

Buckeye Trail

PINE LANE TO EVERETT ROAD
COVERED BRIDGE
4.1 MILES
HIKING TIME – 2 HOURS
ELEVATION CHANGE – 150 FEET
RATING – EASY

RIVERVIEW ROAD

CUYAHOGA RIVER

VALLEY RAILWAY

LOCK 27

EVERETT ROAD
COVERED
BRIDGE

EVERETT ROAD ℗

TO
BATH ROAD

FURNACE RUN

HUNT
FARM

BOLANZ ROAD

At the bottom of this road you join the present State Route 303 and get a short tour of Peninsula. There is much to see in this small canal town. In 1974 the Department of the Interior designated the entire village a national historic district. Peninsula includes a number of historic homes (private) and commercial buildings. If you walk about two blocks off the Buckeye Trail, up to Riverview

60

Road, you pass several historic buildings. South on Riverview Road is the Peninsula Library and Historical Society which contains a good collection of local history. Here you can also enjoy the Mural of Transportation in the Cuyahoga Valley—a stone mural on the face of the library giving a unique bird's-eye view of the area around Peninsula.

Since the early 1900s Peninsula has attracted artists and that tradition is continued today. Several shops and galleries in town offer the works of local craftsmen and women. A bicycle shop and restaurants take care of other visitor needs. Water and public restrooms are available at the Lock 29 Trailhead one block north of State Route 303. For a more complete tour of Peninsula, pick up the walking tour map available in any of the shops.

Back on the Buckeye Trail, follow the blue blazes on State Route 303 across the Cuyahoga River to Canal Street. Turn south, past the historic Fox House, now housing the Cuyahoga Valley Scenic Railroad office. Trail signs direct you down Canal Street, across the bed of the canal, and onto the towpath. Follow the Ohio & Erie Canal Towpath Trail until you reach Everett, about 3 miles south. Along the way you will pass Deep Lock, Lock 28, the deepest lock on the Ohio & Erie Canal. (See Towpath Trail, page 34, for more detail on this area.)

The Buckeye Trail leaves the towpath a short ways south of Lock 27, just before the bridge across Furnace Run. Go west towards Riverview Road, cross the road, then follow it to the intersection with Everett Road. At this point the Buckeye Trail turns west (left) and is routed along Everett Road.

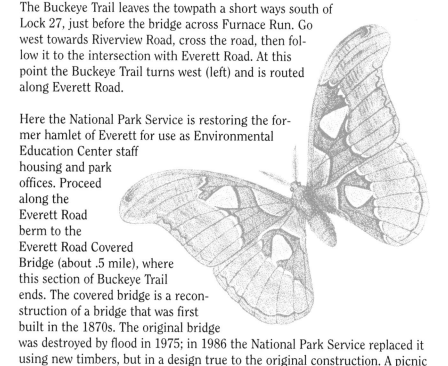

Here the National Park Service is restoring the former hamlet of Everett for use as Environmental Education Center staff housing and park offices. Proceed along the Everett Road berm to the Everett Road Covered Bridge (about .5 mile), where this section of Buckeye Trail ends. The covered bridge is a reconstruction of a bridge that was first built in the 1870s. The original bridge was destroyed by flood in 1975; in 1986 the National Park Service replaced it using new timbers, but in a design true to the original construction. A picnic table and small parking lot are located near the bridge.

61

Everett Road Covered Bridge to Indian Mound Trailhead

The Buckeye Trail from Everett to Bath Road begins along lightly traveled roads, then enters the woods at Ira Road, and ends at Bath Road after passing through O'Neil Woods Metro Park. The trail goes past Hale Farm and Village, operated by the Western Reserve Historical Society. You can tour the homestead, one of the earliest brick houses in this area, dating to 1826, and other Western Reserve style buildings in the village (fee charged). Craftsmen demonstrate skills used in the valley in the 1800s. The historic site also offers refreshments and a picnic area.

Park at the Everett Road Covered Bridge, on Everett Road, .5 mile from Riverview Road. The southern terminus of this section of trail is at Bath Road, near the intersection of Riverview Road. Suggested parking is at Indian Mound Trailhead on Riverview Road, south of Bath Road. A short walk on the Ohio & Erie Canal Towpath Trail connects the trailhead to Bath Road and the Buckeye Trail.

Begin by crossing the covered bridge, then turn left onto Oak Hill Road. This tree-lined road passes private residences, then brings you into view of Hale Farm and Village.

Continue past Hale Farm to the intersection of Oak Hill and Ira Roads. The cemetery here contains graves of many of the early valley families. Also buried here is William Birdsell, the first Superintendent of Cuyahoga Valley National Recreation Area. Follow Ira Road as it passes Old Trail School (an independent coeducational PK-8 school). Just after reaching the intersection with Martin Road, the trail leaves Ira Road to the right and enters the woods, continuing south. The trail begins to climb and takes you into a heavily wooded section of property that was acquired by the park service in the 1990s. Up until then this land was owned by Sherman O. and Mary Schumacher who purchased it from the Botzum family, descendants of early settlers. Sherm Schumacher built miles of graveled jeep roads throughout his farm and delighted in taking visitors on wild rides through the woods. The Buckeye Trail follows some of these jeep roads, and you will notice others intersecting along the way.

While still high on the west ridge of the valley, the Buckeye Trail leaves the former Schumacher property and enters O'Neil Woods, a unit of Metro Parks, Serving Summit County. Here, after crossing a meadow, the Buckeye Trail joins the Deer Run Trail. Follow the trail to the right, north, towards the parking lot and Lone Pine picnic area. Continue past the parking lot and watch for where the trail again enters the woods. Descend to Bath Road, cross, and continue on the Buckeye Trail as it follows Deer Run Trail across a stream and past a meadow, then along Yellow Creek. Some very large sycamore trees line the creek and

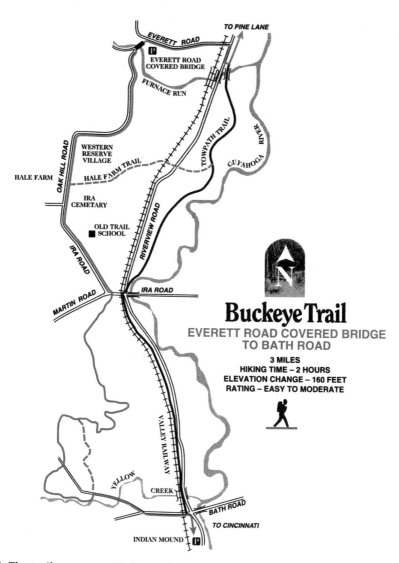

trail. The trail returns to Bath Road a short ways southeast of where it crossed earlier. The Buckeye Trail turns right, leaving Deer Run Trail, and follows Bath Road east. You will cross a bridge over Yellow Creek then reach the intersection with Yellow Creek Road. The historic Botzum cemetery is just off the trail, up Yellow Creek Road to the right. The Buckeye Trail continues on Bath Road to Riverview Road, a crossroads formerly known as Botzum.

At Bath Road the Buckeye Trail leaves CVNRA, beckoning you on. From here it continues south into Sand Run Metro Park and on around the state following canals, trails, and country roads. If you go on following the blue blazes, you will eventually return to this point!

From Rail to Trail

Bike & Hike Trail

Most of the Bike & Hike Trail runs just outside the boundary of Cuyahoga Valley National Recreation Area along the east rim of the valley. Metro Parks, Serving Summit County, maintains a total of 23 miles of Bike & Hike Trail, including two southern legs which lead away from CVNRA to Kent and Stow. Cleveland Metroparks maintains several miles of trail north of Highland Road. Only the 9.8 miles of trail nearest CVNRA are described here.

The beauty of this trail is that the entire length, except for 1 mile, is separated from road traffic, allowing you a quiet and safe ride on even the busiest of traffic days. The trail was one of the first "rails-to-trails" conversions in Ohio, utilizing abandoned railroad beds combined with utility rights-of-way. Following the railroad routes, the trail takes you through some surprisingly remote areas, yet is never more than a mile or two from a crossroad.

Separated from car traffic, the trail is ideal for family bike rides. For the most part, it is surfaced with compacted, crushed limestone, which works well for most bikes and is aesthetically pleasing. (Metro Parks, Serving Summit County has asphalt paving on the section that goes to Kent.) Grades are gentle, 3% or less. There is access to the trail and limited parking at road crossings. Please do not block the gates: park vehicles need ready access for maintenance and emergencies. The best access points are noted on our trailhead map.

You can combine paved roads with the Bike & Hike Trail to make longer loop rides without retracing your route. Also, midway along the trail, there is a connector down to the Ohio & Erie Canal Towpath Trail, offering even more options for loop rides. Just remember, what goes down must come up!

Some sections of the Bike & Hike Trail follow the former route of the New York Central Railroad (originally the Pittsburgh and Lake Erie Railroad). Other sections follow the old "Alphabet Railroad"—the Akron, Bedford, & Cleveland Railroad that carried commuters from Akron to Public Square in Cleveland. That line merged with other electric railroads to form Northern Ohio Traction and Light Company, now known as Ohio Edison. The Bike & Hike Trail in Summit County, which opened in 1972, is the result of a cooperative effort between Ohio Edison and Metro Parks, Serving Summit County, with Metro Parks leasing the right-of-way and maintaining the trail. Cleveland Metroparks developed the northern sections of trail in cooperation with The Illuminating Company.

A mixture of woods, meadows, and wetlands border the trail for its entire length. In July and August you can search for wild berries growing in the

65

unshaded patches between the woods and the path. If you stop and look closely, you can find delicious wild strawberries in June, all the more delicious for their tiny size and the challenge in finding them. But watch out for poison ivy! It thrives along the edges. The ditches along the rights-of-way host cattails, and in some wet areas you can even find watercress. One of our largest summer wildflowers, the common mullein, grows in the sunny borders of the trail. Common mullein can grow up to 6 feet tall and is recognized by its flannel-textured leaves and yellow flowers.

Your chances of seeing wildlife along the trail are good, especially in the early morning. Deer and rabbits may cross in front of you, and birds feed along the shrub edges, along with colorful butterflies and dragonflies.

Bike & Hike

ALEXANDER ROAD TO NESBITT ROAD

2 MILES
BIKING TIME – 15 MINUTES
HIKING TIME – 1 HOUR
ELEVATION CHANGE – MINIMAL
RATING – EASY

DUNHAM ROAD

TO
EGBERT ROAD VIA
ALL PURPOSE TRAIL

ALEXANDER ROAD

SAGAMORE'S CREEK

SAGAMORE ROAD

VALLEY VIEW ROAD

NESBITT ROAD

Starting at the north end, you can access Cleveland Metroparks Bike & Hike Trail on Alexander Road, just west of Dunham Road, where there is a small trailhead parking lot. The Cleveland Metroparks All Purpose Trail also begins here, offering you a paved path heading north through Bedford Reservation. The Bike & Hike Trail goes south on a crushed limestone path, following the New York Central Railroad right-of-way.

The section between Sagamore Road and State Route 82, 2.5 miles, is less scenic than the rest of the trail, as it goes beneath high-voltage electric transmission lines. But even in these areas the surrounding vegetation provides pleasant scenery and wildlife habitat. At State Route 82 there is room for parking several vehicles. Use caution when crossing this busy highway.

The trail continues south on the railroad grade and soon crosses Holzhauer Road. Here there is an option for connecting to the Ohio & Erie Canal Towpath Trail if you wish to plan a side trip or round trip. To do so, follow Holzhauer Road south until it ends. Go onto the crushed stone path which then bears to the right. This connector trail is a steep downhill, ending at the Ohio & Erie Canal Towpath Trail. It uses a short portion of the Old Carriage Trail, a hiking and cross-country ski trail. Note that bicycles are not permitted on the rest of the Old Carriage Trail.

Bike & Hike
NESBITT ROAD TO BOYDEN ROAD

2.5 MILES
BIKING TIME – 20 MINUTES
HIKING TIME – 1.25 HOURS
ELEVATION CHANGE – MINIMAL
RATING – EASY

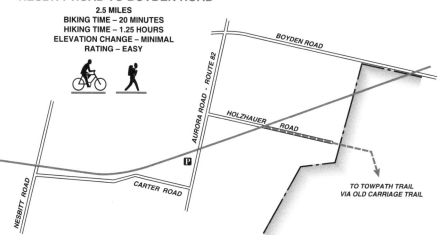

If you do not take the option to the Ohio & Erie Canal Towpath Trail, continue on the Bike & Hike Trail, following the railroad grade, to Boyden Road, then on to Highland Road, where there is space along the road to park a couple of cars. At Highland Road, you leave Cleveland Metroparks jurisdiction and enter Metro Parks, Serving Summit County. There are now milepost signs at each road crossing.

The next road intersection is Brandywine Road, where there is a small parking pull-off. Here the trail must leave the right-of-way and travel on Brandywine Road for 1 mile in order to cross I-271. Turn right onto the roadway to stay on the bike route. Midway along this mile stretch, you pass The Inn at Brandywine Falls, a lovely bed and breakfast in an historic farmhouse. The innkeepers are George and Katie Hoy (see Appendix). Just beyond the inn is Stanford Road. You can leave the bike route here temporarily to reach the Brandywine Falls Trailhead, just around the corner on Stanford Road. The trailhead has restrooms and picnic tables and is the start of the boardwalk leading to Brandywine Falls.

Bike & Hike

BOYDEN ROAD TO HINES HILL ROAD

2.8 MILES
BIKING TIME – 25 MINUTES
HIKING TIME – 1.5 HOURS
ELEVATION CHANGE – MINIMAL
RATING – EASY

Back on Brandywine Road, continue on the Bike & Hike Trail route until you reach the sign directing you back onto the railroad grade. There is parking for about two or three cars here. In .8 mile you cross Hines Hill Road, then in the next section you cross the Ohio Turnpike on a bridge exclusively for the Bike & Hike Trail, just before reaching Boston Mills Road. Just to the west of the trail you can find an ample parking lot, the Bike & Hike Trailhead.

Continuing south, you finish the last 1.7 miles of trail through the most beautiful section of the old railroad cut. Here the trail is deeply shaded and passes between huge sandstone boulders, the remains of the Boston Ledges. Most of the ledges and rock caves were buried under tons of fill used to level out the railroad grade as it traversed a deep ravine. You can rest on a bench placed here near the huge, fern-covered rocks, a cool and especially welcome oasis on a hot summer day. There is private property on either side of the trail, so please limit your exploring to the right-of-way itself.

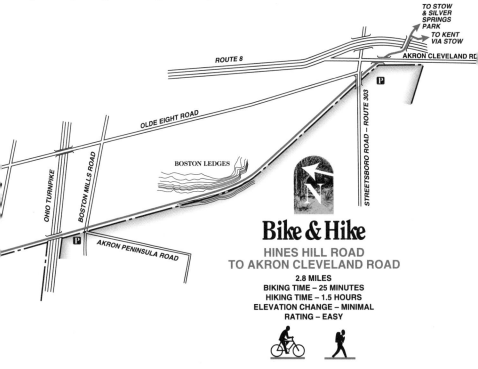

Bike & Hike
HINES HILL ROAD
TO AKRON CLEVELAND ROAD
2.8 MILES
BIKING TIME – 25 MINUTES
HIKING TIME – 1.5 HOURS
ELEVATION CHANGE – MINIMAL
RATING – EASY

Continuing south, you soon go under State Route 303 and reach the ramp up to Akron Cleveland Road. There is a road from the trail to Akron Cleveland Road alongside a motel. Food and water can be obtained at the restaurant nearby. There is no official parking here; however, there is parking at the next road crossing to the south, .75 miles away at Barlow Road. South of the intersection of State Route 303 and Akron Cleveland Road, the trail leaves the edge of CVNRA and soon splits into two legs, one ending in Stow and the other in Kent. Contact Metro Parks, Serving Summit County, for further information on those sections.

69

Construction of RR Trestle across Tinkers Creek c. 1911

Bedford Reservation

Bedford Reservation is a unit of Cleveland Metroparks. The main natural feature of this park is beautiful Tinkers Creek Gorge, a National Natural Landmark. The reservation protects much of the dramatic gorge and in turn creates a delightful place to picnic, hike, ride horseback, or explore for waterfalls.

Tinkers Creek, the largest tributary of the Cuyahoga River, was named in memory of Joseph Tinker, a member of Moses Cleaveland's 1796 surveying party. Tinker was one of three men who died when their boat was capsized in a storm on Lake Erie. Tinkers Creek drops 90 feet in two miles, cutting a steep walled gorge from 140 to 190 feet deep. The inaccessibility of the gorge was a natural impediment to development in the 1800s, except for the more shallow upper gorge where numerous mills were built around the Great Falls of Tinkers Creek in Bedford. These mills ushered the industrial age into the area around 1820, while the rest of the gorge largely escaped timbering and development.

The upper Tinkers Creek Gorge used to be known as the Bedford Glens and was a destination for weekend outings as early as the turn of the century. A popular dance hall was part of Bedford Glens Park until 1944, when the hall burned to the ground ending that romantic era. The gorge first achieved official park protection when Cleveland Metroparks acquired 1300 acres in the 1920s, and later expanded the reservation to 2154 acres.

This unique natural area has many tree and shrub species, an unmatched spring wildflower display, and carpets of ferns, mosses, lichens, and liverworts. Here geology is laid before you as the water-cut gorge exposes all the bedrock found in the valley. Delta-like deposits of red muds and offshore deposits of grey muds and silts constitute the Bedford Formation. Other formations that are exposed here are Chagrin, Cleveland, and Bedford Shales and Berea Sandstone. Winter transforms this gorge into an icy wonderland. The park's more than 70 cascades and waterfalls freeze into ice formations, some 30 to 50 feet high.

The scenic overlook on Gorge Parkway offers a vista (especially in the fall) that many claim is unrivaled anywhere north of the Smoky Mountains. Other attractions of this area include Bridal Veil Falls, Shawnee Hills Golf Course, several picnic areas and shelters, plus ballfields and playfields. The trails of Bedford Reservation are Bridal Veil Falls Trail, Hemlock Creek Loop Trail, the Bridle Trail, the All Purpose Trail, and part of the Buckeye Trail (described in the Buckeye Trail chapter).

Numerous other informal trails have been used over the years as more adventurous visitors explored along Tinkers Creek and its tributaries in search of Bedford Reservation's hidden treasures. In some areas, trails that were constructed years ago are no longer formally used or kept in repair. One such trail runs along the north rim of Tinkers Creek and offers some beautiful views into the gorge, as well as access to hemlock-lined side creeks and small waterfalls. It is permissible to explore these informal trails; remember, however, they are not signed or maintained.

To reach Bedford Reservation from the west, turn onto Dunham Road from Turney Road, Tinkers Creek Road, or Alexander Road. The entrance into the Hemlock Creek Picnic Area is at the intersection of Dunham and Tinkers Creek Roads, and Gorge Parkway is just across Tinkers Creek.

Gorge Parkway and Egbert Road provide access from the east. Egbert Road intersects with Broadway Avenue (State Route 14) near the intersection of State Routes 8 and 14 in Bedford. From Egbert Road, turn onto Gorge Parkway to enter the reservation. Parking is available at either end of the reservation; you can find additional parking along Gorge Parkway and at the Gorge Overlook and Bridal Veil Falls areas, and at Lost Meadows and Egbert Picnic Areas. Picnic tables, grills, restrooms, water, and shelters are available at the major picnic areas, and a Cleveland Metroparks Ranger Station is located at the east end of the reservation at the corner of Egbert Road and Gorge Parkway. Your options for exploring Bedford Reservation are as varied as the many access points to them!

All Purpose Trail

This paved, 8-foot wide, multi-purpose trail offers access to Bedford Reservation's many attractions and accommodates a variety of uses including bicycling, walking, and jogging. The surface is suitable for wheelchairs, however, some grades are relatively steep. Horses are not permitted on the All Purpose Trail, but the Bedford Bridle Trail parallels the route of this trail. A fitness trail is located along the All Purpose Trail near the Egbert Picnic Area.

From the All Purpose Trail you can reach Tinkers Creek Gorge Scenic Overlook and Bridal Veil Falls. The trail crosses two major streams on bridges; the topography varies from level to hilly. Other natural features along the way include hemlock ravines, oak-hickory forests, beech-maple forests, and waterfalls.

You can park at the northeast end of the reservation at Egbert Picnic Area and at the south end at Alexander Road Trailhead. There are several other smaller parking areas along the way. At the south end, the All Purpose Trail links to the Bike & Hike Trail; continuing on the bike trail, you can go farther south along the edge of CVNRA and beyond, to Kent, 28 miles away. At the north end, the All Purpose Trail goes beyond the Egbert Picnic Area for 1 mile to Broadway Avenue in Bedford. In Bedford, Cleveland Metroparks is constructing an all-purpose trail which parallels Hawthorn Parkway, to link this area to South Chagrin Reservation.

Within Bedford Reservation, long loop hikes can be made, if walking, by using the All Purpose Trail in one direction and the Buckeye Trail in the other direction. Bicycles are not permitted on the Buckeye Trail. The All Purpose Trail is easy to follow as long as you just follow the paved surface. It stays mostly within sight of the park roads and is accessible from many points along the way.

Picnic tables, grills, restrooms, water, and shelters are available at the major picnic areas. A Cleveland Metroparks Ranger Station is located at the east end of the reservation at the corner of Egbert Road and Gorge Parkway.

Starting from the east end, at Egbert Picnic Area, begin by paralleling Gorge Parkway on the north side of the road. Cross over to the south side before the entrance road to Lost Meadows Picnic Area. A side trip could be made down to Lost Meadows.

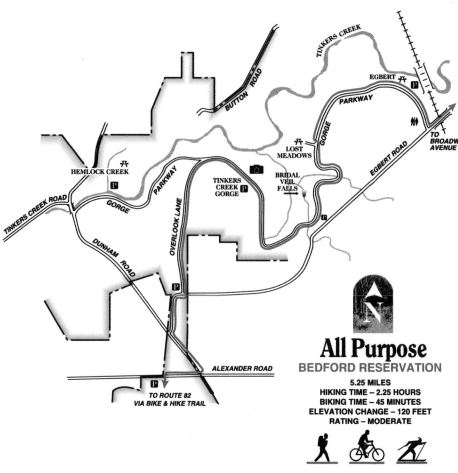

All Purpose

BEDFORD RESERVATION

5.25 MILES
HIKING TIME – 2.25 HOURS
BIKING TIME – 45 MINUTES
ELEVATION CHANGE – 120 FEET
RATING – MODERATE

Continue along the south side of Gorge Parkway, crossing a bridge near Bridal Veil Falls. Here another 10 to 15 minute side trip (walking) takes you down the steps to view the falls.

The next major feature you reach is the Tinkers Creek Gorge Scenic Overlook. There is a small parking lot here near the observation platform. Just past the overlook, leave Gorge Parkway and turn south to follow along Overlook Lane. Cross Egbert Road, veer to the west to parallel the curving Egbert Road, then cross the bridle trail and descend towards the intersection of Egbert and Dunham Roads. Just short of Dunham road, make a sharp turn to parallel Dunham Road on the north side.

At the next intersection, where Dunham Road crosses Alexander Road, there is a small trailhead parking lot. You can continue on the All Purpose Trail by crossing Dunham Road and paralleling Alexander Road for a short distance. You reach the terminus at the trailhead on Alexander Road.

Bridal Veil Falls

10/7/17 VERY COOL w/ SANDSTONE CREEK & WATERFALLS

This short trail is located off Bridal Veil Falls parking area on Gorge Parkway, just east of Overlook Lane. A footpath and stairs lead you to overlooks from which you can view the stream and Bridal Veil Falls.

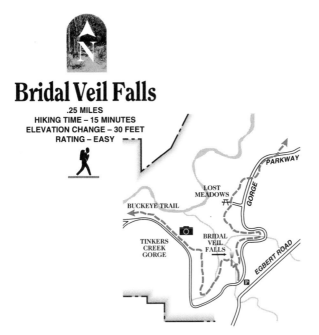

Bridal Veil Falls

.25 MILES
HIKING TIME – 15 MINUTES
ELEVATION CHANGE – 30 FEET
RATING – EASY

PARKWAY

LOST MEADOWS

BUCKEYE TRAIL

GORGE

TINKERS CREEK GORGE

BRIDAL VEIL FALLS

EGBERT ROAD

To begin the trail, cross Gorge Parkway and descend the steps. Follow along the shale-bottomed stream, then cross the stream on a footbridge. Walk a short ways to the last observation platform, this one for viewing the falls itself. From here you can absorb the beauty of the falls and surrounding hemlock ravines.

Part of the Buckeye Trail follows this trail and continues on to the Tinkers Creek Gorge Scenic Overlook to the west and Lost Meadows Picnic Area to the east. From Bridal Veil Falls, you can return to the parking lot via the same route you came on, or follow the Buckeye Trail as your time and wanderlust permit. The hike to the Tinkers Creek Gorge Scenic Overlook passes through a mixed hardwood forest with a spectacular spring wildflower display. Round trip distance is about 3 miles.

Hemlock Creek Loop Trail

This short loop from Hemlock Creek Picnic Area offers you a taste of Tinkers Creek valley from the creek level. You can see the variety of vegetation influenced by the deep valley: hemlocks clinging to the north-facing slope of Tinkers Creek valley contrast with the oaks on the drier south-facing side. In spring, you can find one of the lushest displays of eastern forest wildflowers in CVNRA. Virginia bluebells, wild geraniums, dog toothed violets (including an unusual white variety), phlox, trillium, bloodroot, and hepatica carpet the floodplain soils, delighting amateur botanists. If your interest is geology, you can study the layered history of the valley exposed in the cliff walls. This is also an excellent spot for the birder. Bring binoculars and field guide!

Access to this trail is from the Hemlock Creek Picnic Area, located near the intersection of Tinkers Creek Road and Dunham Road, on the north side of Tinkers Creek. The trail begins beyond the ballfield.

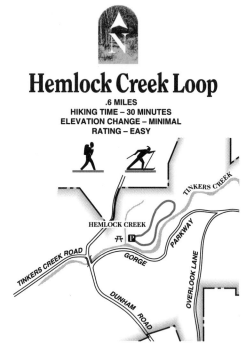

Hemlock Creek Loop

.6 MILES
HIKING TIME – 30 MINUTES
ELEVATION CHANGE – MINIMAL
RATING – EASY

To start the trail, walk away from the parking lot, close to the hillside on your left. Looking ahead and behind, you can see that this alignment used to be an old road. This was Button Road, which still exists at the top of the hill.

It came steeply down into Tinkers Creek valley, and was used by farmers in the 1800s bringing goods to the valley and the Ohio & Erie Canal.

Follow this old road a short distance until the main trail bears to the right. The old road ahead is now just a narrow path. Bear to the right, approaching Tinkers Creek. The trail continues to circle to the right, paralleling the creek. An informal trail goes about 0.8 mile farther upstream, but is no longer maintained. Nonetheless it allows you to explore a little farther up this beautiful creek valley. If you take it, you will know when to turn around when you reach an impassable place in the creek. At that point, return along the same trail to get back onto the loop trail.

Back on the main trail, you will find a couple benches offering a chance to sit and observe. Continuing on the loop, you soon reach the shelter and parking lot where you began. Looking downstream from here you can see the remains of supports for the old Pittsburgh and Lake Erie Railroad (later New York Central, then Penn Central) trestle which crossed Tinkers Creek. High above, on the south side of the valley, you can see the promontory formed by the railroad embankments. The steel trestle was built in 1911, used until the 1960s, then dismantled in 1974. Imagine the scary thrill that many kids must have had, daring each other to cross The Trestle.

Bridle Trail Bedford Reservation

The long Bridle Trail traverses the length of Bedford Reservation, mostly high on the south rim of the Tinkers Creek valley, with one branch which goes south to Sagamore Creek. The trail is partially shared with the Buckeye Trail. Throughout its length it has a wide, firm, stone surface. Traveling the Bridle Trail, you can experience the best of what Bedford Reservation has to offer: deep woods, high ridges, hemlock ravines, Tinkers Creek valley, cascades, and waterfalls.

Trail riding has a long history in the reservation, dating back to the 1920s when the park established the first bridle paths and began using a mounted ranger patrol. You can still find some of the original rock work at culverts and retaining walls along the trail.

The trail is described from the lower (western) end of the Tinkers Creek gorge, where the best parking is located. Park at Hemlock Creek Picnic Area to begin the trail. The picnic area is located off Dunham Road at the intersection of Tinkers Creek Road, at the west end of the reservation. The entrance road crosses over Hemlock Creek just north of where it flows into Tinkers Creek. The Bridle Trail begins at this point, near the bridge—a sign marks the start of the trail. (Look carefully, as the sign is somewhat obscured and off the side of the road).

Begin the Bridle Trail by fording Tinkers Creek to the south side. (This is not passable at high water: in that case, go back out to Dunham Road and cross, with caution, the narrow bridge over Tinkers Creek).

At the opposite bank, climb the short grassy slope onto the berm of Gorge Parkway. Follow the road to the left about 100 feet, then cross the road to where the trail is visible as it starts up a ridge. As you climb this ridge, you can see an old railroad embankment to the right when the leaves are off the trees; the creek valley lies below and to the left.

At the top of this climb, keep towards the edge of the ridge, bearing away from the embankment. The trail sweeps around to the north to follow the curve of the ridge, crossing a side drainage, allowing views of the Tinkers Creek valley when the trees are bare. Follow the trail as it curves and fairly soon you reach an intersection with the Buckeye Trail. The Bridle Trail splits north and south, sometimes sharing the path with the Buckeye Trail. Here you make a choice to either stay along the rim of Tinkers Creek Gorge or turn south to reach the

Bridle Trail
BEDFORD RESERVATION
6 MILES
RIDING TIME – 2.5 HOURS
ELEVATION CHANGE – 270 FEET
RATING – MODERATE TO DIFFICULT

Sagamore Creek valley. We'll first describe the section of trail which continues along Tinkers Creek Gorge.

At the intersection, turn to the left, continuing in a northerly direction through a scenic section along the steeply sloped gorge. Here the trail is shared with the Buckeye Trail, marked with blue blazes on the trees. Near Overlook Lane, bear to the east, leaving the Buckeye Trail, and cross Overlook Lane near the intersection with Gorge Parkway. Parallel the parkway, then cross it near the Tinkers Creek Scenic Gorge Overlook. Now on the north side of Gorge Parkway, rejoin the Buckeye Trail and move away from the road into a mature woods of oaks, hickories, and beeches.

About 1 mile from the overlook you come to Bridal Veil Falls on a tributary of Deerlick Creek. To the left is the falls overlook; the trail bears to the right crossing the creek by ford or footbridge. Steps to the right lead up to Gorge Parkway. The Bridle Trail and Buckeye Trail stay in the woods following the ravine of Deerlick Creek. Both skirt close to the road to get across to the other side of the ravine. This section is exceptionally beautiful, with hemlocks along the creek and waterfalls and rock tumbles below.

Cross the access road to Lost Meadows Picnic Area, go through another forested section, then cross Gorge Parkway. Here you follow along the south side of Gorge Parkway, with Shawnee Hills Golf Course to the right. Cross Gorge Parkway again, along with the Buckeye Trail, then cross the All Purpose Trail, and reenter the woods. The Egbert Picnic Area is to the right. For several miles now you have been high above Tinkers Creek. To reach the creek, continue downhill on the stone path. At the bottom of the hill is the site of the old Powers Mill and some stone remains. This section of trail ends at Tinkers Creek. Now at creek level you can get close to the rushing water that continues to carve the shale-lined gorge. Use the same path to return to the Egbert Picnic Area on Gorge Parkway. The Bridle Trail leaves Bedford Reservation to the east, continuing towards South Chagrin Reservation.

To follow the southern spur of the Bridle Trail, turn right at the intersection where the two sections split. Following this leg of the Bridle Trail south you parallel Overlook Lane, but out of sight of it, for about 1 mile until you reach Egbert Road. The Buckeye Trail shares the route for most of the way. Cross Egbert Road, continue south to Dunham Road, then Alexander Road.

Bridle Trail – Pinery Narrows

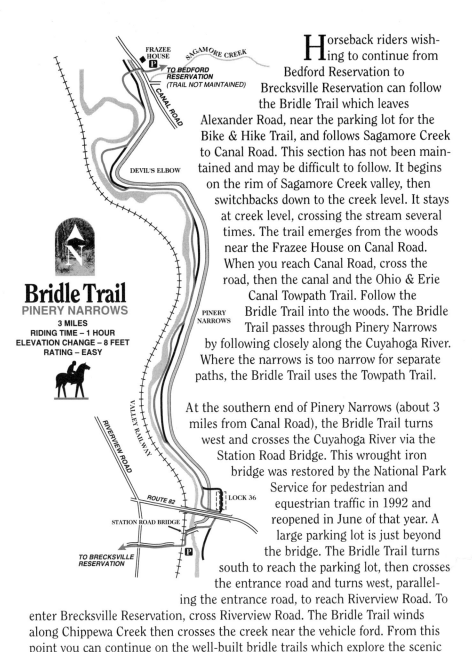

FRAZEE HOUSE

SAGAMORE CREEK

TO BEDFORD RESERVATION
(TRAIL NOT MAINTAINED)

CANAL ROAD

DEVIL'S ELBOW

Bridle Trail
PINERY NARROWS
3 MILES
RIDING TIME – 1 HOUR
ELEVATION CHANGE – 8 FEET
RATING – EASY

PINERY NARROWS

VALLEY RAILWAY

RIVERVIEW ROAD

ROUTE 82

LOCK 36

STATION ROAD BRIDGE

TO BRECKSVILLE RESERVATION

Horseback riders wishing to continue from Bedford Reservation to Brecksville Reservation can follow the Bridle Trail which leaves Alexander Road, near the parking lot for the Bike & Hike Trail, and follows Sagamore Creek to Canal Road. This section has not been maintained and may be difficult to follow. It begins on the rim of Sagamore Creek valley, then switchbacks down to the creek level. It stays at creek level, crossing the stream several times. The trail emerges from the woods near the Frazee House on Canal Road. When you reach Canal Road, cross the road, then the canal and the Ohio & Erie Canal Towpath Trail. Follow the Bridle Trail into the woods. The Bridle Trail passes through Pinery Narrows by following closely along the Cuyahoga River. Where the narrows is too narrow for separate paths, the Bridle Trail uses the Towpath Trail.

At the southern end of Pinery Narrows (about 3 miles from Canal Road), the Bridle Trail turns west and crosses the Cuyahoga River via the Station Road Bridge. This wrought iron bridge was restored by the National Park Service for pedestrian and equestrian traffic in 1992 and reopened in June of that year. A large parking lot is just beyond the bridge. The Bridle Trail turns south to reach the parking lot, then crosses the entrance road and turns west, paralleling the entrance road, to reach Riverview Road. To enter Brecksville Reservation, cross Riverview Road. The Bridle Trail winds along Chippewa Creek then crosses the creek near the vehicle ford. From this point you can continue on the well-built bridle trails which explore the scenic interior of Brecksville Reservation.

81

Dedication of the
Harriet Keeler Memorial

Brecksville Reservation

Brecksville Reservation is the largest reservation of Cleveland Metroparks, encompassing 3090 acres of diverse parkland. It is located near the intersection of State Routes 82 and 21. The first parcels of land were acquired for Brecksville Reservation in 1920, just three years after the establishment of the Cleveland Metropolitan Park District. In 1921 the park board passed a resolution to create the 300-acre Harriet L. Keeler Memorial Woods. In 1935, during the Great Depression, the Civilian Conservation Corps (CCC) established a camp in the reservation in order to construct trails and other facilities. The CCC camp operated through 1937, when it then moved to the Akron Metropolitan Park District's Sand Run Metro Park in Akron.

Chippewa Creek cuts a deep gorge along the northern boundary of this reservation. Seven other ravines are formed by streams working their way to the Cuyahoga River. Therefore there are plenty of hills to climb and streams to cross when you explore Brecksville Reservation. Steep cliffs, huge boulders, and cascading water typify the gorge area. You will find a variety of other natural features throughout the rest of the reservation, including oak-hickory forests, beech-maple forests, shady hemlock ravines, floodplains, and a restored tallgrass prairie. Cleveland Metroparks is using natural resource management techniques to maintain the young chestnut trees in the park and to enhance the oak forests. They are also maintaining habitat diversity by managing old fields, reclaiming apple orchards, and enhancing wetlands.

At either end of this reservation, near the entrances, are several often overlooked, but fascinating, trees. Located near the corner of State Route 21 and Valley Parkway, and again near the intersection of Chippewa Creek Drive and Riverview Road, are groves of dawn redwoods. These trees are often called living fossils because they thrived 100 million years ago in the age of dinosaurs. During the 1940s they were discovered still growing in a remote valley in China. They have now been cultivated through seeds and cuttings.

These dawn redwoods are ancient relatives to our western giant sequoias (thus the Latin name *Metasequoia glyptostroboides*). They differ, however, by being deciduous, dropping their lacy leaves in autumn. You can recognize them by the pyramidal shape, horizontal branches, and grayish bark which is deeply fissured and reddish.

Brecksville Nature Center, one of the oldest buildings in the park district, is a good place to begin your visit to the reservation. Located on Chippewa Creek

Drive, near the north entrance to Brecksville Reservation, the nature center is staffed by naturalists and has natural history exhibits. The WPA (Works Progress Administration) built the center in 1939, using local building materials: American chestnut trees killed by the chestnut blight in the 1920s and 30s and Berea sandstone quarried in the reservation. The center is listed on the National Register of Historic Places.

Most of the trails in Brecksville Reservation radiate out from the nature center area. The trails include the Buckeye Trail, several hiking trails ranging from .25 to 4 miles long, a paved all purpose trail, and bridle trails. Brecksville Reservation also offers golfing at the 18-hole Sleepy Hollow Golf Course. In the winter, good snow permits cross-country skiing on the golf course and trails, and snowmobiling in an area along Chippewa Creek Drive.

A series of different colored markers designate the various hiking trails in Brecksville Reservation. Although the trails are well-marked, at times you will be following several trails and markers at once, which can be disconcerting until you are more oriented to the system. All color-coded trails, except the Buckeye Trail and the spur off My Mountain Trail, follow a circular pattern, returning you to your starting point if you follow any one color marker. You can connect several of the loop trails to create even longer hikes. All the trails are described in the following pages except for the Buckeye Trail, which is described in the Buckeye Trail section.

The main access to Brecksville Reservation is via Valley Parkway, off State Route 21, 1.25 miles south of State Route 82. A second entrance, Chippewa Creek Drive, is off State Route 82, just east of State Route 21. Yet a third entrance is from Riverview Road: Chippewa Creek Drive intersects Riverview Road just south of State Route 82.

Classroom at the Nature Center

All Purpose Trail

The All Purpose Trail in Brecksville Reservation is an asphalt-paved, multi-use trail. It has several access points and two branches, and is suitable for cycling, jogging, or hiking. The northern branch basically follows along Chippewa Creek Drive from Riverview Road to the Chippewa Creek Trail parking area. The southern leg leaves Chippewa Creek Drive just west of the vehicle ford across Chippewa Creek. It follows Valley Parkway to the western boundary of the reservation, at State Route 21. Part of the All Purpose Trail includes a 1.4 mile physical fitness trail, located near the Chippewa Creek ford in the northeast corner of the reservation.

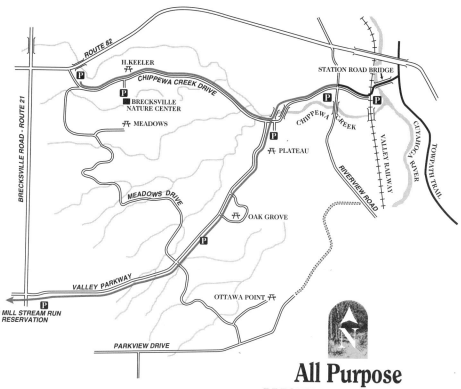

All Purpose

BRECKSVILLE RESERVATION

4.5 MILES
HIKING TIME – 2.25 HOURS
BICYCLING TIME – 40 MINUTES
ELEVATION CHANGE – 410 FEET
RATING – EASY TO MODERATE

To begin from the north entrance into the reservation, start at the Chippewa Creek Gorge parking area, located on Chippewa Creek Drive just south of State Route 82. The paved path leaves from this parking area. As you begin, you pass the scenic overlook on the left, then the short spur to the Harriet Keeler Memorial on the right. Shortly past this, you pass the Harriet Keeler Picnic Area on the left, and access to Brecksville Nature Center and other trails to the right. Continue east along the road, going up and down several hills along the way, down to the floodplain of Chippewa Creek and the intersection with Valley Parkway. The Chippewa Picnic Area is on the right on the south side of the road. You can continue on the All Purpose Trail across Chippewa Creek, past a parking area and playfields, to finish at Riverview Road. It is here that you also find a physical fitness trail complete with exercise stations. Across Riverview Road, a paved trail leads to the Station Road Bridge Trailhead. From there you can access the Ohio & Erie Canal Towpath Trail, a multi-purpose trail surfaced with crushed limestone.

The southerly leg of the All Purpose Trail (1.9 miles) climbs the hill alongside Plateau Picnic Area, paralleling Valley Parkway, and crosses the Buckeye Trail near the entrance to Oak Grove Picnic Area. Further along, heading southwest, it intersects with the Bridle Trail and again with the Buckeye Trail as you approach the Deer Lick Cave area.

Cross Meadows Drive and continue along Valley Parkway; Sleepy Hollow Golf Course is to the north. You come to the end of the All Purpose Trail in Brecksville Reservation at State Route 21.

Chippewa Creek Trail

Chippewa Creek Trail begins by following the southern edge of the gorge formed by Chippewa Creek, then crosses Chippewa Creek Drive and shares a return route with the Deer Lick Cave Trail. Chippewa Creek has cut a remarkable gorge in the 12,000 years since the retreat of the last glaciers. The bedrock geology of the Cuyahoga Valley is easily visible here, exposed in the cliffs of the gorge.

Chippewa Falls, located under the State Route 82 bridge, is formed as the creek falls over Berea Sandstone onto the more easily eroded Bedford Shale. The creek itself is littered with huge blocks of stone, eroded off the walls of the valley. You can view the falls by taking a short side trip off the main trail. A parking lot just south of State Route 82 allows close access to the falls viewing area.

We suggest that you begin the Chippewa Creek Trail from the paved parking lot at the Brecksville Nature Center, located on Chippewa Creek Drive a half mile from State Route 82 . Green hiker symbols on the trees mark the trail. Here it is described in a clockwise direction, beginning along Chippewa Creek.

From the parking lot in front of the nature center, begin by crossing the road and entering the Harriet Keeler Picnic Area. Turn left on the paved All Purpose Trail. Turn right where the Chippewa Creek Trail leaves the All Purpose Trail. Look for the green markers to stay on the Chippewa Creek Trail. For awhile the green markers are joined by the white markers of the Scenic Overlook Trail Now approaching the gorge, you reach a small overlook shelter. From here you can view the beautiful gorge and the creek cascading over huge boulders far below.

Continue on the Chippewa Creek Trail through a hemlock woods. Hemlocks are evergreens of rocky, cool, shady areas. You can recognize them by their pyramid shape and flat needles which have two white lines on their undersides.

In a little while, a shelter is visible through the woods to your right. You now begin a gradual descent along the edge of the gorge. The trail splits; take the right fork and continue downhill through tulip trees, oaks, and beeches. Continue this descent to the floodplain of Chippewa Creek. A marshy area is to your left.

Cross a stream on a wooden footbridge; Chippewa Creek is soon visible on the left. Cross another stream on a small suspension bridge. This bridge was built by the 26th Engineering Company of the Ohio National Guard from Brook Park in April 1981. An open area provides another view of the creek.

Now you reach Chippewa Creek Drive—cross the road, heading towards the small picnic area. The trail now shares a return route with the Deer Lick Cave Trail (red markers) along the south side of the road. Walk parallel to the road, then cross a small stream on stepping stones. Soon you begin a climb up out of the valley. A trail splits off to the right as you bear to the left, following the edge of the ridge with views of the stream below. The presence of cinnamon ferns and hemlocks suggests a cooler microclimate as you approach the cascade of the stream. The trail also passes some huge white and red oaks. A number of sandstone slump blocks can be seen below the cliffs.

The Chippewa Creek and Deer Lick Cave Trails join with the yellow-marked Valley Stream Trail. The combined trails lead to Brecksville Nature Center. From the center, again follow the green-marked Chippewa Creek Trail as it joins the main paved entrance walk back to the parking lot.

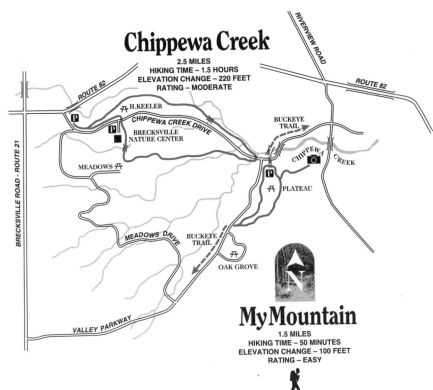

My Mountain Trail

My Mountain Trail climbs one of the many ridges in Brecksville Reservation, providing vistas of the beautiful surrounding hills and valleys. The deep forest and carpet of moss lends a feeling of a Tolkien fantasy to the experience. You half expect a troll or elf to appear from behind a tree!

The main access to this orange-marked trail is from Plateau Picnic Area, off Chippewa Creek Drive. The picnic area includes a shelter and small parking lot.

To begin the trail from the parking lot, face the shelter and look for the row of large sycamores just to the right of the paved path. The orange markers on these trees mark the start of the trail. Begin by climbing a steep ridge paralleling Valley Parkway. This levels out to a plateau; a vernal pool lies to the left of the trail. Mature oaks and beeches, and an occasional hemlock, make up the woods along the way. To the right is a nice vista of the next ridge; here you get a sense of the rolling topography formed by the side creeks flowing to the Cuyahoga River.

To continue on My Mountain Trail, turn left where it joins the Buckeye Trail (blue blazes). Stay with the orange markers to continue on My Mountain. Again, there are beautiful views of the adjacent forested ridges.

My Mountain Trail and the Buckeye Trail continue through the woods. Close to the Plateau Picnic Area, a spur of My Mountain Trail goes to the right to another ridge. Along this spur trail you pass large white oaks and more scenic vistas. A slump along this steep hillside has opened up a view to the north, and in winter, you can see in the distance the State Route 82 bridge over the Cuyahoga Valley. Return on the same spur to the main trail, then turn right and descend off the plateau towards the picnic area. Walk up the Plateau Picnic Area entrance drive to finish the hike.

Scenic Overlook Trail

This short trail, marked with white symbols, leads to the Harriet Keeler Memorial and an overlook of Chippewa Creek Gorge. Start the trail on Chippewa Creek Drive at the parking area with the sign "Harriet Keeler Memorial Woods and Memorial." Begin by walking the short distance to the memorial, a large glacial erratic boulder set in a shady grove within the 370-acre Harriet Keeler Memorial Woods. A bronze plaque on the rough rock has a profile of Keeler and an inscription: "Harriet Keeler 1846-1921, Teacher-Educator-Citizen. She liveth as do the continuing generations of the woods she loved."

Born in Kortright, New York, Harriet Louise Keeler graduated from Oberlin College in 1870. She moved to Cleveland where she taught in the Cleveland Public Schools until 1878. She continued with the school district, eventually rising to Superintendent in 1912. In 1913 she earned a Doctor of Laws degree from Western Reserve University. Keeler was active in the suffrage movement and served as president of the Cuyahoga County Suffrage Association. She wrote her first book, Studies in English Composition, *in 1892 and continued writing until near the time of her death. She published eleven books, mostly on nature.*

The Cleveland Metropolitan Park Board, in a resolution passed in 1921 to commemorate the life and services of Harriet Keeler, stated, ". . . the interest in the great outdoors and its woods and fields, so encouraged and promoted by the books of that gifted writer and educator, is so in keeping with the spirit and purpose of the Cleveland Metropolitan Park Plan" that "a suitable tract. . . shall be set aside to be known as The Harriet L. Keeler Memorial Woods" to be "planted with native trees, shrubs and flowers described in the writings." The memorial was erected in 1923 and was rededicated in 1990.

Continue on the Scenic Overlook Trail by following the white markers past the memorial, bearing to the right. Cross Chippewa Creek Drive and join with the All Purpose Trail for a short distance. Watch for where the Scenic Overlook Trail leaves the All Purpose Trail and drops directly towards the overlook. From here you can enjoy good views of Chippewa Creek Gorge and the waterfall, framed by graceful evergreen hemlock trees clinging to the steep slopes.

Follow the Scenic Overlook Trail along the rim of the gorge for a short distance. Watch for where the trail bears to the right to direct you back up the hill to Chippewa Creek Drive. Cross the All Purpose Trail and the road to return to your car. You can easily combine this trail with the green-marked Chippewa Creek Trail or the yellow-marked Valley Stream Trail for longer hikes.

Valley Stream Trail

Valley Stream Trail starts from Brecksville Nature Center and passes through several habitats: coniferous and deciduous woods, a tallgrass prairie, and stream ravine. A paved, accessible portion near the start of the trail has interpretive signs. There is parking for the nature center and trails on Chippewa Creek Drive; follow the paved trail to the center.
Valley Stream Trail is marked with yellow hiker symbols on the trees.

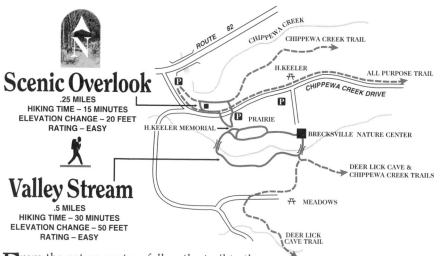

Scenic Overlook

.25 MILES
HIKING TIME – 15 MINUTES
ELEVATION CHANGE – 20 FEET
RATING – EASY

Valley Stream

.5 MILES
HIKING TIME – 30 MINUTES
ELEVATION CHANGE – 50 FEET
RATING – EASY

From the nature center, follow the trail to the west (right) of the center into a spruce planting. Adjacent is a tallgrass prairie restoration project that has been developed by now retired Senior Naturalist Karl Smith and his staff. An elevated deck with signs illustrating 31 prairie species is at the eastern edge of the planting. The trail continues along the south end of the prairie as you approach the Harriet Keeler Memorial. See the Scenic Overlook Trail chapter for a description of the memorial and the surrounding area. The Scenic Overlook Trail (white markers) leads to the right to reach a view of Chippewa Creek.

Valley Stream Trail goes to the left, leaving the memorial area. The ground cover here is myrtle. Descend on steps to the stream bed. Several large oaks are nearby and a wooden bench offers a peaceful place to rest. Cross the stream on a bridge, then climb back up the small ravine. Meadows Picnic Area can be seen in the distance.

The trail descends again to the stream and another bridge crossing and intersects with Deer Lick (red) and Chippewa Creek (green) Trails. Continue up the hill to the nature center. The Valley Stream Trail connects all the trails near the Brecksville Nature Center: Scenic Overlook Trail (white markers), Chippewa Creek Trail (green markers), and Deer Lick Cave Trail (red markers).

Deer Lick Cave Trail

Deer Lick Cave Trail is one of the longer loop trails in Brecksville Reservation. It crosses several valleys, small streams, and high ridges, with the unusual sandstone formation of Deer Lick Cave being its major feature. This is a good choice for a long, rugged, and scenic hike.

Deer Lick Cave Trail begins at Brecksville Nature Center, where there are parking and restrooms. (The nature center is located on Chippewa Creek Drive, about .5 mile south of State Route 82.) Deer Lick Cave Trail can also be reached from the southern end, beginning at Deer Lick Cave itself, off Valley Parkway. The trail is marked with red symbols on the trees. It is described in a counterclockwise direction.

Begin Deer Lick Cave Trail at the Brecksville Nature Center. Turn left as you face the center, passing the small outside amphitheater. Descend through the forest, then cross the stream on a wooden bridge and take the steps to the left. (Valley Stream Trail, marked with yellow, branches off to the right before the steps). This section of Deer Lick Cave Trail is also shared with the green-marked Chippewa Creek Trail.

At the top of the steps, turn right. Skirt the edge of a pine planting as you come to Meadows Picnic Area. Cross a gravel road and the paved access road, turn right at the Bridle Trail, then left to descend to a stream valley. There is a spring, with signs of iron deposits, on the left. The trail crosses the stream on a footbridge next to the Bridle Trail ford. A very large white oak is on the left of the trail as you approach another ford and bridge; the trail then climbs out of this creek valley and skirts the edge of a large meadow.

When the trail splits just past the meadow, take the right fork, downhill. Continue down along the edge of the stream, then cross it on a bridge. There is an interesting shale formation where two streams converge near the bridge. The trail climbs out of this valley to Meadows Drive. Turn left at Meadows Drive to follow it 100 yards, then cross and enter a red pine planting.

The next small stream valley is also crossed via a bridge; this is a lovely sight in winter, when you can clearly see the trail curving down and around to cross the creek. Climbing from this valley, you can see Sleepy Hollow Golf Course to your right. The trail again drops to cross another stream. The Buckeye Trail now joins from the right (blazed in blue). Follow the red markers to the left as you approach Meadows Drive and cross it again (leaving the Bridle Trail).

Take Deer Lick Cave Trail to the left, then descend stone steps to the sandstone formation for which the trail is named. Here you'll find sandstone ledges, shelter caves, and waterfalls, with abundant mosses and large rocks. Cross the stream three times on footbridges to reach the main cave, on your left.

The trail climbs out of this valley, paralleling Valley Parkway; a short spur trail leads to the right and up to an overlook of the Deer Lick Cave area. On the main red-marked trail, shared with the Buckeye Trail, you reach a kiosk telling the story of the Buckeye Trail, with mileages to each terminus in three directions. This is about the half-way point of the Deer Lick Cave Trail hike. You can find water and restrooms a little farther on at the Oak Grove Picnic Area to the east, across Valley Parkway.

Deer Lick Cave Trail descends down wooden steps and crosses a stream on a bridge. The Buckeye Trail goes off to the right near here. Stay on Deer Lick Cave Trail, following the edge of the ridge, where you get good views of the surrounding woodlands to the left. Gradually you descend through beeches and tulip trees to reach Chippewa Creek Drive and a small picnic area.

At this point, the green-marked Chippewa Creek Trail shares the same return route west to the nature center. Follow both trails to the left, just south of Chippewa Creek Drive. After crossing the entrance drive to the picnic area, continue on the south side of the road about 200 yards. The trail continues into

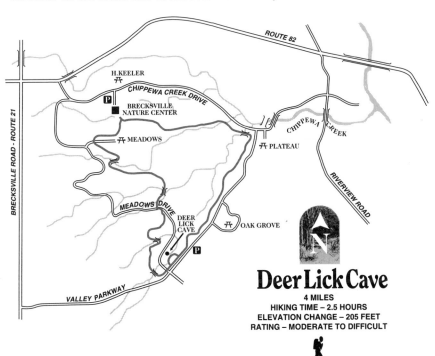

Deer Lick Cave

4 MILES
HIKING TIME – 2.5 HOURS
ELEVATION CHANGE – 205 FEET
RATING – MODERATE TO DIFFICULT

the woods at this point, then across a small stream on stepping stones before beginning a climb out of the valley. The Bridle Trail splits off to the right, as you bear to the left, following the edge of the ridge, with views of the stream below. Cinnamon ferns and hemlocks do well in the cooler microclimate of the stream ravine. Large white and red oaks line the trail.

The red and green-marked trails join, then leave, the Bridle Trail near Meadows Picnic Area. Shortly after this, you retrace the route you started on. Cross a boardwalk over a wash as the trail approaches the back side of the nature center. Descend steps to the right for the final stream crossing, then climb the hill to finish the trail.

Options here for longer hikes include going on to the Valley Stream Trail and the Tallgrass Prairie or crossing Chippewa Creek Drive to complete the rest of the Chippewa Creek Trail.

Buckeye Trail Crossroads – Brecksville

Bridle Trail – Brecksville

The Bridle Trail in Brecksville Reservation winds through some of the most scenic and remote areas in the reservation. The trail consists of a large figure-eight loop plus a small loop around the Brecksville Stables. A continuation of the trail leaves the reservation to the west, following the metroparks' parkway. Another bridle trail connection goes east from Brecksville Reservation following Chippewa Creek Drive to Riverview Road and on into the Station Road Bridge Trailhead. From here one can ride north towards Bedford Reservation.

The Bridle Trail in Brecksville Reservation is wide, well-graded, and surfaced with gravel. All along the way you can see the Civilian Conservation Corps' fine stonework on culverts, bridge abutments, and retaining walls.

The trail can be reached from the stables located on Meadows Drive off Valley Parkway. A concessionaire operates the stables, providing boarding and riding lessons but no rental horses. There is parking for cars and trailers at the stables. Parking is also available at the National Park Service's Station Road Bridge Trailhead off Riverview Road, south of State Route 82.

The short loop behind the stables and the longer trail can all be reached by riding to the right of the stables along the pasture towards the woods, or to the left of the stables, just inside the woods. The short loop simply makes a circle around and behind the stable area, in the woods, and is mostly level. It skirts near private property on the west and south sides.

To take the longer ride, start out on the trail to the left of the stables. A trail from the stable drive leads into the woods and soon branches—the trail straight ahead goes around the stable; the trail to the left begins the longer trail. Follow this out to Meadows Drive, cross the drive and enter the woods. Here you are sharing the trail with the Buckeye Trail. The trail parallels Meadows Drive; a branch of the bridle trail joins on the left. Descend to cross a creek—Meadows Drive can be glimpsed to the left, crossing the creek on an arched sandstone bridge.

As the Bridle Trail approaches Valley Parkway, bear to the right to parallel the All Purpose Trail and the road. Here the Buckeye Trail leaves and crosses the road. Staying on the Bridle Trail, swing away from the road into a woods of tall oaks and hickories. A large ravine opens out on the right. The trail follows this ravine edge around, then comes back out to the All Purpose Trail. Cross the All Purpose Trail, then the road, and intersect with the Buckeye Trail and Deer Lick Cave Trail on the far side of the road. The three trails share the same path for a short distance.

While the Buckeye Trail stays near the road, the Bridle Trail turns left and begins a steep descent into a beautiful, wide, creek valley. At the bottom, ford the creek and continue in the valley. The steep wooded hills to either side give a secluded feel to this lush, dished valley. It is in this bottom land that you come to an intersection, the middle of the figure-eight: the outer loop of the Bridle Trail continues straight ahead in the valley, while to the left (west) a short-cut connector trail follows a creek upstream to join the western side of the big loop. You can take this branch for a short ride back to the stables.

To continue on the longer loop, stay in the creek valley following the trail to the point where it joins the Deer Lick Cave and Chippewa Creek hiking trails (marked in red and green respectively). For a short way, all three trails share the same path. (Note that a bridle trail also goes to the right (east) here, leading to Riverview Road. It continues across Riverview Road and into Pinery Narrows, linking Brecksville Reservation to the Bridle Trail in Bedford Reservation.) Bear to the left, paralleling Chippewa Creek Drive, cross a creek, then begin a gradual climb. The hiking trails split off to the left, while the Bridle Trail bears to the right. Cross another creek, this time on a bridge, go straight ahead, then wind out around a knoll and up onto a ridge. Another scenic creek valley is now on your left. Hemlock trees intermingled with tall oaks and hickories are especially attractive in the winter.

Follow the Bridle Trail down to the left, across the creek, then back up. Again the Bridle Trail meets up with the hiking trails, as all go out towards the fields at Meadows Picnic Area. To stay on the Bridle Trail, cross the field to the diagonally opposite corner.

At the far side of the field, enter the woods and soon join the Deer Lick Cave Trail again. The trail curves down into a ravine where you can cross the creeks via footbridges, or ford them if on horseback. Climb out of this valley; at the top you find the trail bordered by a ravine to the left and an extensive meadow on the right.

An unofficial trail takes off to the left; both the bridle and hiking route go to the right and take you back down to the creek bottom. Along the way the trail is edged by an old stone retaining wall. At the bottom you reach the intersection with the trail that joins the east and west portions of the big loop.

The main loop of the Bridle Trail bears to the right and crosses a bridge; look to the right to see the rocky confluence of two branches of the creek. Climb out of this valley towards Meadows Drive. Turn left at Meadows Drive to follow it 100 yards, then cross. On the opposite side you go immediately into a planting of red pines.

Just beyond, the trail winds in graceful curves as it drops to cross a creek, then climbs again to within sight of Sleepy Hollow Golf Course. Beyond the golf course, as you approach Valley Parkway, you again cross the Buckeye Trail. The Deer Lick Cave Trail turns left with the Buckeye Trail, but you proceed straight ahead to cross the parkway, then the All Purpose Trail. In a short distance, you reach an intersection: the crossing trail is a bridle path leading to State Route 21 to the west (where Valley Parkway extends west to connect with Mill Stream Run Reservation) and back across Meadows Drive to the east. Go straight ahead to return to the stables.

Before reaching the stables, you will come to another intersection where the loop behind the stables leaves to the right. Bear left to reach the parking lot. The loop behind the stables is short, level, and goes through an attractive fantasy-land spruce woods. It ends at the east end of the parking area, near Meadows Drive.

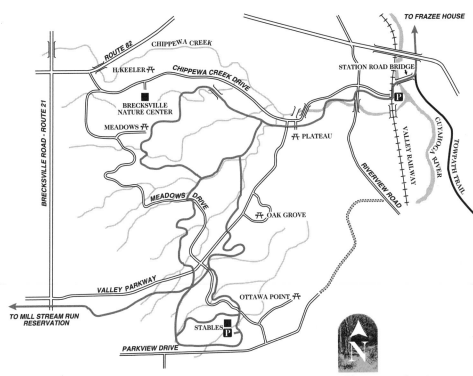

Bridle Trail
BRECKSVILLE RESERVATION
9 MILES
RIDING TIME – 3 HOURS
ELEVATION CHANGE – 260 FEET
RATING – MODERATE TO DIFFICULT

Brandywine Falls Boardwalk c. 1900

Jaite / Boston

The Jaite/Boston area is, in more ways than one, the heart of the 33,000 acre federal recreation area. Here public and private lands intertwine. All three park agencies have jurisdiction here-Cleveland Metroparks, Metro Parks, Serving Summit County, and the National Park Service. Privately owned recreation facilities include two downhill ski areas and a water park.

Cuyahoga Valley National Recreation Area's headquarters is housed in the former company town of Jaite. Built from 1907 to 1924 to house millworkers who worked at the Jaite Paper Mill, the town's buildings have been adaptively restored for offices. The parking lot across from the main headquarters building used by park staff during the week can also be used as an alternative trailhead for weekend trail users. An interpretive wayside exhibit, located on a small knoll just east of the park headquarters, tells the story of Jaite.

Boston is a small community that, during its canal heyday, was reported to be larger than Cleveland. Just north of Peninsula, it too was an ideal half-way point to overnight on the boat trip from Akron to Cleveland. It was from a boatyard in Boston that the *Allen Trimble* was launched on July 3, 1827, signaling the opening of the Ohio & Erie Canal. All the buildings in Boston are private, except the Boston Store which now houses a canal boat building exhibit and is well worth a visit.

Brandywine Falls c. 1890

Trails in the Jaite/Boston area offer something for everyone who loves the outdoors: scenic hemlock ravines, waterfalls, mature forests, cool creekside bowers, steep climbs and descents, and opportunities to make longer outings by using the Ohio & Erie Canal Towpath Trail along with the other trails.

Old Carriage Trail

Winding stretches of trail which border deep, wooded ravines make up most of the 3.25 miles of the Old Carriage Trail. These nearly level miles are anchored at both ends of the trail by invigoratingly steep sections. Three bridges, ranging in length from 150 to 166 feet, carry you across three of the ravines midway along the route. These features, along with beautiful vistas across the Cuyahoga River valley, make this trail one of the most enjoyable and challenging for skiing or hiking.

The Old Carriage Trail is located on the eastern side of the valley in the area between State Route 82 and Highland Road. This area has had a significant history in the Cuyahoga Valley, from the time of early Native Americans to the present. It is believed that Native Americans found the area suitable for encampments. After white settlers came, the high ground of Northfield Township was settled for farming, then, with the coming of the canal, rough roads led down to the canal boat loading areas. At one time, Holzhauer Road extended further south than it does now, connecting the farms to a canal boat loading station at the foot of Red Lock Hill.

In the late 19th century, Wentworth G. Marshall and his wife Louise purchased 1000 acres of farmland in this area, bordered generally by Northfield Road, Holzhauer Road, and the canal. At that time Marshall was establishing himself in Cleveland as a drug store merchant. He bought an interest in a store on the site of the present Terminal Tower in 1876, then established a store at the corner of Superior and Public Square. He went on to create a successful chain of 46 Marshall Drug Stores. Marshall and his two sons all had beautiful homes built in the then just developing Shaker Village (Shaker Heights), but for the summers W.G. Marshall moved his family to their summer home built on his farm called Rocky Run.

Both Wentworth and his son George enjoyed botany and invested much energy into developing an arboretum on the farm. They also planned and built carriage roads throughout the wooded acres, designing them to take advantage of the ridgetops. Large culverts were placed in ravines and covered with fill to eliminate steep ups and downs. The Marshalls also encouraged a summer camp here, called Friendly Inn, which gave city youngsters opportunities for country experiences.

After the Marshalls sold their farm, developers in Northfield began building an open-space development known as Greenwood Village. It was partially completed when it encountered financial troubles. During the early 1980s, a new owner decided to continue the development, however, in the meanwhile the remaining undeveloped acreage had been included within the boundary of the new Cuyahoga Valley National Recreation Area. Just in time, in 1983, the National Park Service purchased 518 acres and the builder went ahead with development outside the boundary of the park.

When the park acquired this property, it also acquired a ready-made trail, the old carriage roads which the Marshalls had built throughout their property. Much of the road system was still in excellent condition, however, in several places the park boundary was drawn across ravines, cutting off portions of the carriage road. This resulted in the necessity of building the beautiful steel box truss bridges that the trail is now known for! As you explore this lovely trail, keep an eye out for evidence of the earlier inhabitants, especially for the Marshalls who so loved and shared their Rocky Run Farm.

The Old Carriage Trail plus a section of the Ohio & Erie Canal Towpath Trail together make a 3.75 mile loop. To reach it from the south end, start at Red Lock Trailhead, located on Highland Road, .5 mile from Riverview Road. To reach Old Carriage Trail from the north, get on the Towpath Trail at Station Road. A round trip from either trailhead is at least 5.3 miles. Please note that the Towpath Trail is a multi-use trail, but the Old Carriage Trail is reserved for hiking and skiing only, except for a southern portion which is designated as a multi-use connector between the Towpath and the Bike & Hike Trail. The Old Carriage Trail is described here from the southern entrance at Red Lock Trailhead. Red Lock Trailhead has parking and a portable toilet, but no water.

From Red Lock Trailhead, follow the Ohio & Erie Canal Towpath Trail north. The old canal basin is on your right. This low lying area provides excellent habitat for wildlife. In the spring, you can hear spring peepers and toads, and wood ducks and great blue herons fly up ahead of you, usually spotting you before you see them. You can also watch for warblers, orioles, indigo buntings, woodpeckers, flycatchers, and many other bird species as well as signs of deer, muskrat, and beaver activity.

Follow the Towpath Trail into a more wooded section, where the overarching trees create a tunnel effect. About .75 mile from the start you reach the intersection of the Towpath Trail and the Old Carriage Trail. Turn right to follow the Old Carriage Trail counterclockwise. (You can also go straight ahead on the Towpath Trail for .5 mile to pick up the northern end of Old Carriage Trail if you wish to do the trail in the reverse direction.)

Turning to the right, cross the canal bed via a wooden bridge. A bench on the bridge provides a pleasant spot for rest or nature watching. From this point, the trail climbs steeply up a section of one of the old roads which is now

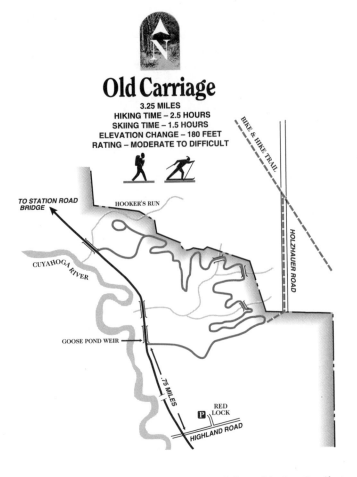

Old Carriage

3.25 MILES
HIKING TIME – 2.5 HOURS
SKIING TIME – 1.5 HOURS
ELEVATION CHANGE – 180 FEET
RATING – MODERATE TO DIFFICULT

TO STATION ROAD
BRIDGE

HOOKER'S RUN

BIKE & HIKE TRAIL

HOLZHAUER ROAD

CUYAHOGA RIVER

GOOSE POND WEIR

.75 MILES

RED
LOCK

P

HIGHLAND ROAD

surfaced for bicycle traffic as well as foot traffic; follow this for .6 mile to reach the top of the ridge, a gain in elevation of 150 feet. This section of trail connects the Towpath Trail to the Bike & Hike Trail. For a short span, you are on a narrow hogback with views to either side. At the top of the ridge you reach a trail intersection. Turn left to continue on the Old Carriage Trail. (The connector trail goes straight to Holzhauer Road.)

Now begin a winding course along the fingers of land projecting between the ravines, following along the east rim of the Cuyahoga Valley. At 1.2 miles from the start of the Old Carriage Trail loop, descend to the first of three single-span steel bridges, Rocky Run Bridge, named after the Marshalls' farm. From here you can see the small stream below rippling over a bed of shale.

After another half mile of winding trail, you reach the second bridge, this one crossing a ravine lined with oaks, maples, and beeches. Two stately oaks at the north end give this bridge its name, Twin Oaks Bridge. Shortly after this, you reach the third bridge, Hemlock Bridge, spanning a lovely hemlock ravine. As you can see from the way the bridges are nestled between the trees, the National Park Service required the use of special construction techniques to install them so that there was minimal disruption to the surrounding woodlands.

Cross-country Skiing on Old Carriage Trail

At this point, you are quite close to the eastern boundary of the national recreation area. You can see homes in the Greenwood Village development to your right. Please respect the private property, and if in doubt as to which way to go, bear to the left, away from the homes but staying on the high ridge.

Continue to follow Old Carriage Trail along the edges of ravines, moving away from the homes and out along a long narrow point of land. Continue generally north, then, on a switchback, descend to cross a short wooden bridge. Past this bridge, you once again come close to the park boundary, then reach the start of the 170-foot descent to the Towpath Trail. Just after you begin your descent, a short loop trail branches off to the right (for skiers this serves as an emergency runaway ramp!); this trail leads to a bench—perfect for lunch or quiet contemplation. Back on the main trail, it's all downhill from here!

At the bottom of the hill, rejoin the Towpath Trail. Turn left (south) to complete the loop. (Turn right if you want to add some mileage along the Towpath Trail). The canal is now on your left; the Cuyahoga River is to the right, at one point cutting in close to the trail. Just before you reach the point where you first left the Towpath, cross a bridge built upon the old abutments of a canal structure known as Goose Pond Weir.

Continue straight ahead to finish your ski or hike, unless you'd like to go around a second time! In .75 mile you reach the end of your tour at Red Lock Trailhead.

Stanford Trail

Stanford Trail connects the Stanford House Hostel to the Brandywine Gorge Trail and Brandywine Falls. Although relatively short, the trail has several steep sections, making it more challenging than it may first appear. Allow plenty of time for this trail as there is much to discover. The gorge and falls of Brandywine Creek provide a dramatic scenic reward at the upper end of the trail, midway a short spur trail leads to a woodland pond, and nearly the entire trail is surrounded by a mature hardwood forest. Double the time allowed for this hike if you do not leave a car at Brandywine Falls.

There is also a short trail from the hostel to the Ohio & Erie Canal Towpath Trail. Find this trail just across Stanford Road, opposite the lower end of the hostel driveway. From the Towpath Trail you can go north or south and make connections to other trails, including the Buckeye Trail, making Stanford House Hostel an excellent hub from which to explore the valley.

The name of the hostel and trail derives from an early settler. In 1806 James Stanford arrived as part of a surveying crew from the Connecticut Land Company. He settled in the valley and became a prosperous farmer and community leader in Boston Township. His son George built the home which is now Hosteling International's Stanford House Hostel.

Much of the land you cross on the Stanford Trail once belonged to Waldo L. Semon. He, a surveyor himself as well as a noted inventor, became interested in the history of the area. He reported in a monograph that this area is transected by David Hudson's trail, one of the earliest travel routes in this part of the valley. In 1799 David Hudson left Connecticut for the wilderness of Ohio, traveling mostly by water, as overland routes were plagued with difficulties. Going from Lake Ontario to Lake Erie, he eventually reached the mouth of the Cuyahoga River. Hudson traveled upstream until his way was blocked by shallow water and rapids. This "Hudson's Landing" is located near the confluence of Brandywine Creek and the Cuyahoga River. From this point he set out over land to locate his Western Reserve holdings, an area which is now Hudson. He most likely followed Indian trails southeasterly towards the high ground in Hudson Township. This route became the earliest road in the area.

Stanford Trail was cleared by the Cleveland Hiking Club (CHC), which has since adopted this trail. Further improvements, including the construction of several bridges, have been made by CHC, the Cuyahoga Valley Trails Council, and several Eagle Scouts.

This trail begins at the Stanford Trailhead located behind the Stanford House Hostel. The hostel is on Stanford Road about .75 mile north of Boston Mills Road. You will find a small parking lot behind the barn for trail users and hostel guests. The trail ends at Brandywine Falls, a beautiful destination for lunch. There are picnic tables, grills, and restrooms at the Brandywine Falls end of the trail.

Start the Stanford Trail at the bulletin board at the northeast corner of the parking lot. Follow the mowed paths through the old pasture, towards Stanford Run. Just before the creek, a short loop trail intersects to the right and left. Cross the creek on a bridge, then wind through the woods. Fairly soon, bear to the left to begin the climb up the hill. The trail was rerouted here to lessen the steepness of the climb and reduce erosion. Some casual trails along the way have been blocked off by brush; be careful to keep to the main trail.

Part way up the hill the trail skirts around a small ravine, then later follows the edge of a larger ravine. Some of this route follows long established trails, in places edged by some domestic flowers planted by former landowners. Cross the second ravine on a small boardwalk. Soon after this boardwalk you reach the historic David Hudson trail. Turn to the left along the historic route for about 50 yards, then turn to the right.

For a side trip, you can stay on the David Hudson Trail and go north to reach Averill Pond. Stu Averill, son-in-law of Waldo Semon, owned a farmstead on Stanford Road just north of the current Stanford House Hostel. Mr. Averill constructed the pond in the early 1950s and stocked it with bass and bluegill. The Averills enjoyed many family picnics along the pond's shores and over the years documented the great variety of wildflowers growing throughout the surrounding woods.

Follow the spur trail back to the intersection with Stanford Trail to continue on to Brandywine Falls. Continue on the Stanford Trail, now lined with large beech trees, descending towards another creek valley. Steps help you down the steep slopes, and bridges make the creek crossings easy.

Just before the climb back out of the valley, the Stanford Trail intersects with the Brandywine Gorge Trail. You can follow the Brandywine Gorge Trail as an alternate route to reach Brandywine Falls, if the stepping stones placed in Brandywine Creek are passable. At the intersection of these two trails, the Stanford Trail continues up a steep slope, made easier by a long set of steps constructed by CVTC volunteers. At the top of the hill the trail leads from the more mature forest into younger growth and finally into a utility right-of-way. Cross the right-of-way and go onto Stanford Road. Walk along the road for about 200 yards until you reach the Brandywine Falls boardwalk. The scenic reward for your efforts lies just beyond.

The National Park Service has built a wonderful series of stairs and observation platforms to provide a close-up view of 65-foot Brandywine Falls. Hemlock, maple, and black locust trees surround the walkways which incorporate two observation decks and benches. The upper part of the boardwalk, the picnic area, and restrooms are all accessible to those using wheelchairs.

The upper walkway (750 feet long) is poised along the rim of the gorge and leads to the remains of a grist mill and factory. It is beautiful here in any season—in spring and summer the boardwalk is cooled and obscured by leafed-out trees; sugar maples light the gorge in gold and yellow in fall, and in winter, ice formations along the gorge are spectacular. (Parts of the boardwalk may be closed at times in winter if icy conditions make the footing hazardous.)

The lower walkway and stairs (300 feet long), hugging the rock-walled ravine, lead to a lower observation deck where you might get showered by waterfall mist if the water is running high. For good reason the falls have become a favorite for artists and photographers as well as many wedding parties (permit required) looking for a romantic backdrop! Take your time to enjoy the sounds of cascading water and the spectacular views. If you are in the area in the latter part of May, you will be treated to the heavenly scent of the black locust trees in bloom. It's delightful!

On the north side of Brandywine Creek is the Wallace farm, circa 1848, which is now The Inn at Brandywine Falls. This bed and breakfast, operated by innkeepers George and Katie Hoy, is a delightful place to stay while exploring CVNRA. The Hoys lease the buildings from the National Park Service through the Historic Property Leasing Program. They have restored the farmhouse and barn and filled the rooms with 19th century style furnishings, many of them made in Ohio.

After visiting the falls, return to the start of the Stanford Trail using the same route, or continue across the top of the falls and along the north side of Brandywine Creek, following the Brandywine Gorge Trail. One mile from the falls the gorge trail again joins the Stanford Trail.

Brandywine Gorge Trail

*This beautiful trail descends Brandywine Creek gorg_*
*creek, crosses Brandywine Creek below Brandywine F_*
*portion of Stanford Road, and ends at the Stanford Tra_*
*you can make a loop trip by using the Stanford Trail to r_*
Falls Trailhead. However, during high water Brandywine C_ ....sable
and you must return on the same route. Nonetheless the gor_ _pectacular
during high water and the trail is worth the hike down and back up via the
same path. Delicate wildflowers in the spring, cool shade in summer, dramatic
fall color, and winter ice formations make this gorge a great destination any
time of the year.

The Brandywine Gorge Trail was built almost entirely by Cuyahoga Valley
Trails Council volunteers during 1992 and 1993, and was dedicated on
National Trails Day, June 5, 1993. The final, essential link was accomplished
by the National Park Service trail crew when they placed large sandstone step-
ping stones for the creek crossing. The route partially follows a former farm
road cut into the side of the ravine just behind the historic Wallace farm, now

...ywine Falls. Undoubtedly there is much hidden history here ...to the heyday of the village of Brandywine when the mills at the ...re the hub of local activity. The village no longer exists, most of the ...dings having been removed when I-271 was built through the site of the original settlement.

To reach Brandywine Gorge Trail, park at the Brandywine Falls Trailhead located on Stanford Road just west of the intersection with Brandywine Road. Follow the signs to the boardwalk. The National Park Service built the boardwalk, stairs, and observation platforms to provide views of the beautiful gorge and spectacular 65-foot Brandywine Falls. Use the upper deck to reach the old mill foundations at the lip of the falls. Brandywine Gorge Trail begins at the end of the foundations. Cross over the top of the falls on an old road bridge, then follow the north side of the gorge for a short distance, watching for the trail sign behind The Inn at Brandywine Falls. The trail continues on a stone path just behind the inn.

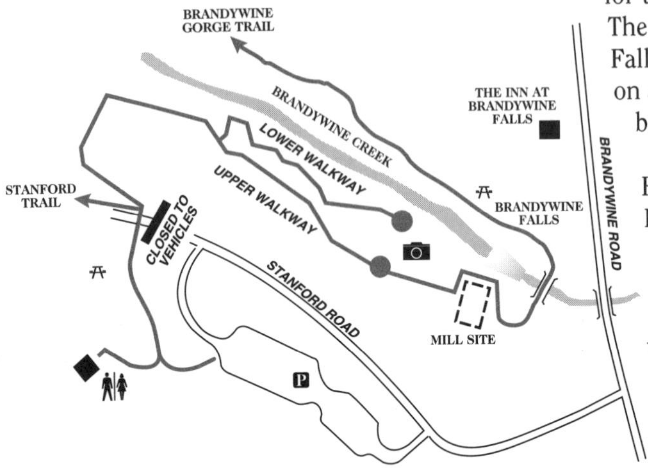

Brandywine Falls Detail

From this point the Brandywine Gorge Trail enters the cool shade of the woods. Dramatic views of the gorge can be seen to the left, especially when the leaves are off the trees. Even when foliage obscures the view you can hear the sound of rushing water far below. Along the rocky rim of the gorge a few large hemlock trees are mixed in with the hardwoods. These gracefully shaped evergreens grow in moist ravines throughout the valley.

Chunks of sandstone of varying sizes line the trail. In a number of places sandstone pieces have been arranged into rock waterbars to keep the trail well drained. Use caution as the stones can be slippery when wet. At the bottom of the hill, descend a few steps and cross a low area on stepping stones. To the right is a small woodland pond formed at the base of a rock ledge, a good spot for amphibians in the spring. After going up a few more steps you will come to a spur trail which leads off to the left. It ends at a shaded bench overlooking a small cascade on Brandywine Creek.

108

On the main trail, continue in the lowlands for a short
rock ledge edging the pond (visible when the leaves are do
oak tree indicates that at one time the surrounding area was
allowing the oak to branch freely and grow larger than any of its
neighboring trees. After the trail winds closer to the creek, it turns
the left and descends to Brandywine Creek. Under normal conditions y
cross the creek on large stepping stones. These sandstone blocks were salv
from old foundations and canal structures throughout the valley and put to us
to carry hikers across the creek. Although the creek is placid most times of the
year, after heavy rains it can move with enough force to displace even these
heavy stones. If the stones are submerged, slippery, or out of place please do
not attempt to cross.

Once across the creek, follow the trail a short distance to Stanford Road. The
trail continues on the other side of Stanford Road, crossing a utility right-of-
way before reentering the woods. Another old oak tree is growing among
younger trees along the east side of the trail.

About 250 yards from Stanford Road, the Brandywine Gorge Trail intersects
with the Stanford Trail. To complete the loop and return to Brandywine Falls,
follow the Stanford Trail up a long set of steps to the top of the hill. At the top,
the combined trail veers to the left and goes onto Stanford Road for the short
walk back to the Brandywine Falls parking lot.

Brandywine Inn

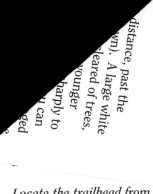

...distance, past the
...wn). A large white
...eared of trees,
...ounger
...harply to
...can
...ed

of the shorter trails in CVNRA, yet offers some
*o lovely waterfalls. The falls are only a quarter
different from each other. Blue Hen Falls is
es a clean 15-foot drop over erosion resistant
Bedford Shale. Downstream, at Buttermilk Falls,
scade over 20 feet of Bedford Shale.*

Locate the trailhead from Riverview Road by turning west onto Boston Mills Road, just south of Boston Mills Ski Resort. Go 1 mile west of the intersection, past the Ohio National Guard buildings; watch for a sign and narrow drive to the right (north). At the end of the short drive is parking for four to five cars. A paved trail leaves from this parking area. For a short distance, the Buckeye Trail shares this paved trail with the Blue Hen Falls Trail. The remainder of the trail is a narrow, rough footpath. Future improvements are planned for the section of trail between the two falls.

Blue Hen Falls

To follow the trail, start out on the paved path. The trail drops from the parking lot and winds down quickly to stream level where it crosses Spring Creek on a bridge. Looking down from the bridge, you can clearly see the Berea Sandstone creek bottom, including fractures in the rock and a pothole formed by rock particles swirling around.

Just past the bridge, the long-distance Buckeye Trail (marked by blue blazes) splits to the left for points north. Follow Blue Hen Falls Trail to the right until you reach the view of Blue Hen Falls.

Blue Hen Falls

1.2 MILES (Round Trip)
HIKING TIME – 1 HOUR
ELEVATION CHANGE – 110 FEET
RATING – EASY TO MODERATE

From here you can see the capstone of sandstone at the head of the falls. This is the result of water eroding back into the shale on the wall of the falls, forming an undercut. At the base of the falls is a plunge pool, a large cavity formed from the force of falling water striking the Bedford Shale below. Mineral deposits under the falls seep from and discolor the surrounding rock. In winter, ice sculptures form along the falls. This is a favored spot for artists, photographers, or anyone who enjoys the serenity of falling water in a woodland setting.

Continuing downstream, follow the narrow footpath, crossing the creek three times, to reach Buttermilk Falls. There are stepping stones above the falls, but in times of higher water be prepared to wade in water 6-8 inches deep. You can view Buttermilk Falls from the lip or from the bottom of the drop. Just before the stream drops over the lip, look for a wall of exposed rock dripping with moisture. Tiny plants, including liverworts, cling to this oozing rock, creating a miniature, emerald garden wall. The moisture from the falls also maintains a carpet of moss along the trail. Please stay on the trail to minimize damage to the area.

Return to the parking area via the same trail, or try some Buckeye Trail hiking as your time allows.

Bathers at Furnace Run Metro Park c.1947

Furnace Run Metro Park

One of the oldest park areas in Summit County, Furnace Run is a unit owned and operated by Metro Parks, Serving Summit County. It is located in Richfield, south of Ohio Turnpike Exit 11 and east and west of I-77. Most of the 889 acres were acquired in 1927 through the generous donation of the family of Charles Francis Brush, Jr. The Akron Metropolitan Park District developed the acreage into a park in the 1930s, employing work relief crews. Brushwood Lake, originally used for swimming, is now enjoyed by wildlife watchers and ice skaters. Owls, herons, warblers, and waterfowl all benefit from the lake and surrounding habitat.

Two place names—Furnace Run and Bog Iron Pond—suggest a history of iron ore in this area. Bog iron is a hydrous iron oxide that was found in wet areas in Summit County. An early history of the area states that iron ore was discovered along Furnace Run valley and that there probably was an iron furnace in the area.

CCC Bench

Reach the Brushwood area of Furnace Run Metro Park via Brecksville Road (marked State Route 21 north of I-77). Just south of the intersection with I-77, turn west onto Townsend Road. The entrance into the park is 1 mile down the road. Metro Parks, Serving Summit County, has remodeled and expanded the attractive pavilion situated on the edge of Brushwood Lake. It formerly served as a bathhouse. The pavilion is enclosed, heated, fully accessible, and has a food service area and restrooms. (The pavilion requires a reservation, while the restrooms remain open even when the pavilion is locked). There are picnic tables, grills, and water along the playing field and along Furnace Run. Three easy trails are located in the Brushwood area: Buttonwood, Old Mill, and Rock Creek Trails. All three can be intertwined to create a pleasant morning or afternoon hike.

You can also reach the H.S. Wagner area of Furnace Run Metro Park from Brecksville Road: less than .5 mile south of I-77, turn east onto Brush Road. This area and its one trail are named for Akron Metropolitan Park District's first director, who once owned the land and planted it with thousands of daffodils.

113

Buttonwood Trail

Buttonwood Trail, in the Brushwood area of Furnace Run Metro Park, is an easy, nearly level trail that makes a clockwise loop around a section of Furnace Run. It is named for the many sycamores, or "buttonwoods" along the way. Sycamores favor the rich bottomlands of rivers and streams and are most noticed for their mottled trunks with patches of peeling bark. But it is their fruit, 1-inch balls hanging on drooping stalks, which gives them the nickname buttonwood.

Reach this trail from the parking lot by going past the pavilion, across a bridge, and through a picnic grove. There you find the trail sign for all three Furnace Run trails. Buttonwood is marked with the pine tree symbol.

Start the Buttonwood Trail along with the Old Mill Trail; both lead off to the right. Beech and maple trees fill the woods here, with the maples lighting the path in autumn with their brilliant yellow leaves. To your right is a marshy area along Furnace Run, a good place to watch for birds. Pass the point where the return loop of Old Mill Trail comes in from the left; Buttonwood Trail continues straight ahead. Shortly after this point is a good view of Brushwood Lake and some signs of beaver activity.

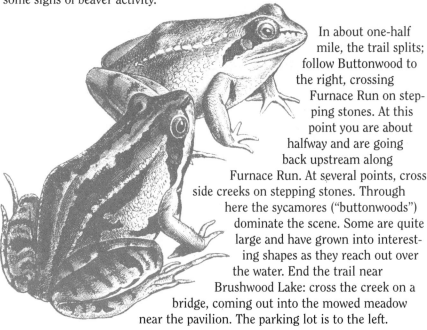

In about one-half mile, the trail splits; follow Buttonwood to the right, crossing Furnace Run on stepping stones. At this point you are about halfway and are going back upstream along Furnace Run. At several points, cross side creeks on stepping stones. Through here the sycamores ("buttonwoods") dominate the scene. Some are quite large and have grown into interesting shapes as they reach out over the water. End the trail near Brushwood Lake: cross the creek on a bridge, coming out into the mowed meadow near the pavilion. The parking lot is to the left.

Old Mill Trail

Old Mill Trail, in the Brushwood area of Furnace Run Metro Park, provides an easy walk along Furnace Run and the ridge above it. Woods of beech and maples surround the trail, with wildflowers at your feet in the spring and the sunshine of golden leaves overhead in the fall. The trail is marked with the Metro Parks symbol of a deer hoof print.

Begin Old Mill Trail from the parking lot of the Brushwood area. Go past the pavilion, across a bridge, and into the picnic grove. Turn to the right; Old Mill Trail and Buttonwood Trail start off together. Fairly soon you come to the point where the return loop of Old Mill Trail comes in from the left; continue straight here, along with Buttonwood Trail.

In a half-mile, the two trails split: go to the left to stay on Old Mill Trail.

OHIO TURNPIKE

ROCK CREEK TRAIL

SHORT CUT

BRUSHWOOD PAVILION

Old Mill

1 MILE
HIKING TIME – 45 MINUTES
ELEVATION CHANGE – MINIMAL
RATING – EASY

Buttonwood

1 MILE
HIKING TIME – 45 MINUTES
SKIING TIME – 30 MINUTES
ELEVATION CHANGE – MINIMAL
RATING – EASY

TOWNSEND ROAD

FURNACE RUN

BRECKSVILLE ROAD

Climb a short, steep slope to reach the ridge above. Years ago a severe storm downed a number of trees on this ridge; they now lie on the forest floor providing food and shelter to numerous insects, birds, and small mammals. Follow the ridge on this return side of the loop. You are traveling north, paralleling I-77. Three side ravines can be easily crossed via stepping stones or bridge.

Just before the trail descends to rejoin Buttonwood Trail, you come to a large boulder commemorating the gentleman who formerly owned the land:

Complete the trail by descending the hill and turning right, returning to your starting point in the picnic grove. You can continue onto Rock Creek Trail for a longer hike.

Rock Creek Trail

Another easy trail in the Brushwood area of Furnace Run Metro Park, Rock Creek Trail follows part of the course of a small tributary of Furnace Run. It's good for family hikes, even with small children, as they love to toddle along next to the creek. If they tire, you can take the shortcut; it is marked with a trail sign and cuts the distance in half. This floodplain area is also great for spring ephemeral wildflowers. Rock Creek Trail is marked with the Metro Parks oak leaf symbol and begins from the picnic grove along with two other trails.

Begin Rock Creek Trail by going across the playing field, past the pavilion, over the creek, and into the picnic grove. A trail sign there directs you to turn left. As you begin Rock Creek Trail, you will likely hear the sounds from I-77, built since this area has been a park. But the creek here commands your attention, as you follow it upstream, crossing it and its many side creeks on wooden bridges. Mature maples, beeches, and other deciduous trees line the trail. Patches of the ancient plant *Equisetum,* commonly called scouring rush, help anchor the sandy soil along the stream banks. The shortcut trail, marked with a trail sign, leads across the creek and back to the playing field.

Rock Creek

1.2 MILES
HIKING TIME – 45 MINUTES
SKIING TIME – 30 MINUTES
ELEVATION CHANGE – MINIMAL
RATING – EASY

SHORT CUT

BRUSHWOOD PAVILION

BUTTONWOOD TRAIL

77

If you do the whole loop, about halfway around you cross the stream and change direction, now heading south. On the return side of the loop, you go through deciduous woods, then a stand of white pines. A lovely picnic area is situated along the creek. Leaving the picnic area, you pass Bog Iron Pond. This pond is slowly but surely losing its pond-ness and taking on the look of a marsh. It was probably dug sometime in the 19th century by bog iron miners for charcoal furnaces in the area.

Complete Rock Creek Trail by following the path out into the playing field above the pavilion. The parking lot is directly ahead, beyond the border of trees.

H.S. Wagner Daffodil Trail

> And then my heart with pleasure fills,
> And dances with the daffodils.
>
> *–William Wordsworth*

The H. S. Wagner Daffodil Trail is a favorite of many hikers of all ages, especially in the springtime. You may find yourself returning year after year to enjoy the welcome color of thousands of daffodils along the 1-mile trail. H.S. Wagner, the Akron Metropolitan Park District's first director, planted the flowers on this property which he had bought for a home site. He never built here, and later sold the land to the park district (now Metro Parks, Serving Summit County), allowing it to be enjoyed by all.

The Daffodil Trail is located in the H.S. Wagner unit of Furnace Run Metro Park on Brush Road, about halfway between Black Road and Brecksville Road. You can reach Brush Road from Brecksville Road, south of where I-77 intersects or by taking Black Road north from State Route 303. There is a small parking lot here but no other facilities.

Begin the Daffodil Trail at the parking lot. The trail starts off wide and level, with hardwoods to either side, passes a row of lovely hemlock trees, then opens out into a grassy area. A bench and a tall old oak tree invite you to rest awhile in this peaceful setting.

Daffodil

1 MILE
HIKING TIME – 45 MINUTES\
SKIING TIME – 30 MINIUTES
ELEVATION CHANGE – MINIMAL
RATING – EASY

From the clearing, the trail begins to make a loop through a relatively level area bounded by two stream ravines. Keep going straight ahead to take the loop in a clockwise direction. Large oak trees and beeches line the ravine that is now visible to your left, while at your feet are the beginning of the many clusters of planted daffodils.

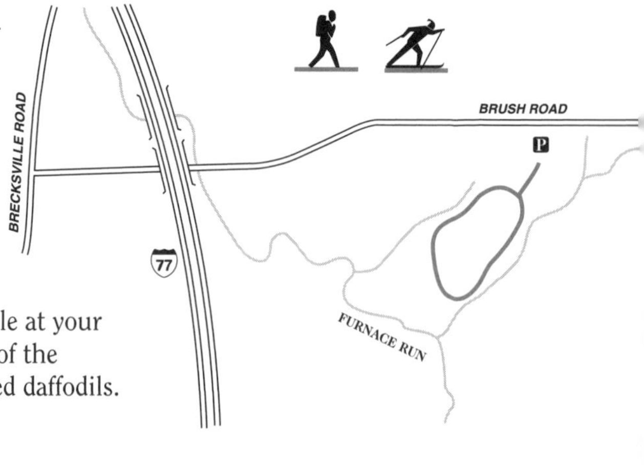

BRECKSVILLE ROAD

BRUSH ROAD

77

FURNACE RUN

118

The tributary to your left empties into Furnace Run; the trail stays on the high ground above these streams. Where the trail begins to curve around, you may be able to glimpse Furnace Run flowing through the wide valley below. This is about the halfway point; continuing on around you come to the other tributary valley which bounds this trail. Again, large, older trees line the trail and slopes, including some tall shagbark hickories, obvious by their loose, "shaggy" bark. The hickories, oaks, and beeches that you see through here are all indicative of a mature woods. The area to the right, however, has much younger trees, indicating the area was a clearing not long ago.

To complete the loop, follow the path back into the grassy clearing. A couple of American holly trees stand out among the plants edging the grass. Bear to the left to follow the trail back to the parking lot.

On the Daffodil Trail

Planting White Pines

Happy Days Visitor Center

Two trails are located in the immediate vicinity of Happy Days Visitor Center: Haskell Run Self-Guided Nature Trail, just to the south of the center, and Boston Run Trail, to the north. Haskell Run Nature Trail is only one-half mile long but connects to the Ledges and Kendall Lake trails, giving you the opportunity to hike for a half-hour or all day.

Before starting on the trails, you may want to get better acquainted with the interesting history of the Happy Days building. Happy Days Visitor Center celebrated its 50th anniversary in 1989. It has not always been a visitor center but has served the public throughout its 50+ years. The area around the center was a Civilian Conservation Corps (CCC) camp during the 1930s when the CCC was constructing trails and shelters in what was then Virginia Kendall Metropolitan Park. The CCC craftsmen constructed Happy Days to house a summer camp for children from the Akron public school system. It was the last and largest building they constructed in the area.

The name for the camp and building derives from the Roosevelt era "Happy Days Are Here Again" song. The building project itself was a joint venture between the Akron Metropolitan Park Board and the National Park Service, with the National Park Service preparing the design and contract documents. Local money ran out before the project was completed, but the Metropolitan Park District's Director, H.S. Wagner, convinced the National Park Service to fund its completion. Little did the NPS know at that time that the fruit of their investments would be returned to them forty years later.

Happy Days Camp continued here until the mid 1940s. From then until 1976, the Akron Metropolitan Park District operated the building as a reservable shelter. In 1974 President Gerald Ford signed the law to create Cuyahoga Valley National Recreation Area. A few years later the management of Virginia Kendall Park was transferred to the new national recreation area. The National Park Service then made improvements to allow for year-round use of the building, and in 1980 Happy Days became the first visitor center in CVNRA.

The building is constructed of wormy chestnut wood and locally quarried sandstone. The many chestnut trees that had thrived in the surrounding forests were all killed in the fungal blight during the 1920s. Ironically, though the trees were killed, they provided an excellent building material, for the wood has exceptional workability, resistance to decay, and a desired rustic appearance. Therefore, all the CCC buildings in Virginia Kendall were built of chestnut wood, including the privies! In this way, the chestnut trees live on.

121

Inside Happy Days Visitor Center, you can visit the Great Hall which formerly housed the camp's school children; be sure to look up at the partial second story. Here the counselors could peek down upon the children in the dormitory. A large oak ice box from the camp's kitchen now sits in the Great Hall.

Happy Days Visitor Center is located on State Route 303, between State Route 8 and Akron Peninsula Road. There are picnic tables and grills near the visitor center and restrooms and water inside. In the visitor center, you will find rangers who can give you information on trails and on the ranger-led programs. The Great Hall often hosts exhibits and programs, and on request you can view the recreation area's introductory slide show. The park's bookstore, operated by Eastern National Park & Monument Association, offers an excellent selection of field guides and other books pertaining to the Cuyahoga Valley and the National Park System. The visitor center is open daily, 8 a.m. to 5 p.m., except for major holidays. During the winter, operating hours are reduced.

Haskell Run Self-Guided Nature Trail

Haskell Run Trail is a short footpath that guides you through a wooded ravine, typical of many such ravines in the Cuyahoga Valley. The route is designed as a self-guided nature trail: for full enjoyment of this trail, look for the self-guiding interpretive booklet located at the trailhead bulletin board near the visitor center.

The trail is located just outside Happy Days Visitor Center and makes a short loop beginning and ending near the center. Happy Days is located on State Route 303, between State Route 8 and Akron Peninsula Road. There are picnic tables and grills near the visitor center and restrooms and water inside.

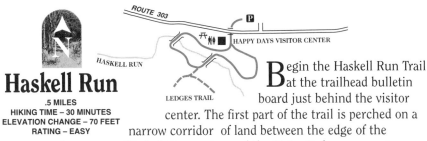

Haskell Run

.5 MILES
HIKING TIME – 30 MINUTES
ELEVATION CHANGE – 70 FEET
RATING – EASY

Begin the Haskell Run Trail at the trailhead bulletin board just behind the visitor center. The first part of the trail is perched on a narrow corridor of land between the edge of the Haskell Run ravine and the Mater Dolorosa cemetery. The cemetery is privately owned and maintained, but you are welcome to visit.

At the junction with a service road, turn to the right onto the service road, and follow it down into the ravine, then downstream along Haskell Run. Water is a prominent feature here. While oaks grow up on the drier ridgetop, down here the water-loving plants, such as mosses, skunk cabbages, and sycamores, thrive. Especially in summer, you can notice the drop in temperature and increase in humidity in this well-shaded valley. In the spring, it's a wildflower garden.

Cross the creek on a bridge; just after this crossing is the intersection with a short trail connecting Haskell Run Trail to the Ledges Trail. Stay down by the creek to continue along Haskell Run Trail. The stream runs year-round and descends 360 feet in 2 miles, emptying into the Cuyahoga River west of here. The surrounding habitat supports a diversity of animals including frogs, salamanders, songbirds, mice, chipmunks, squirrels, raccoons, and deer. In the summer you might hear two of the most beautiful songsters of our deciduous woodlands: the hooded warbler and the veery.

After crossing the creek again, climb back out of the ravine. The trail brings you out at the west end of the large playing field. Crossing the field brings you back to the visitor center.

Boston Run Trail

The Boston Run Trail follows the upper portion of Boston Run and its tributaries. It is mostly in wooded areas, with some parts crossing small patches of fields reverting to woodland. Stands of beech trees with their silver-grey bark and a rocky hemlock ravine add special beauty to this route.

The trail's length and several moderate hills make it a good one for skiers of intermediate levels. Take extra caution here if the snow cover is marginal or icy—the hills are short and relatively steep. A good snowplow maneuver is advisable. When in doubt, sit it out!

The Boston Run Trail follows the route of an earlier motorbike trail which was opened in 1972 by the Akron Metropolitan Park District. In 1978 the park district transferred the entire Virginia Kendall Park area to the National Park Service, making the trail part of the new Cuyahoga Valley National Recreation Area. The badly eroded trail was closed and remained unused for several years until the National Park Service improved it, rerouted some sections, and reopened it as a cross-country ski trail.

To reach this trail, park at the Happy Days Visitor Center parking lot on the north side of State Route 303, less than 1 mile west of State Route 8.

Begin Boston Run Trail at the northeast corner of Happy Days Visitor Center parking lot, near the trailhead bulletin board. The trail is signed in a counterclockwise direction for the pleasure and safety of skiers, taking best advantage of the terrain. Follow the edge of the playing field; go past the exit of the loop trail to find the start of the trail. The trail veers to the left into the woods to begin the loop.

Very soon, begin a steep, curving downhill run. After a short climb and another steep, curving downhill, cross a bridge and begin the climb alongside State Route 303. At the top of this slope the trail winds away from the road through a woodland. There is another short descent, then a section now heading well away from the road through a beech woods, a wet area, and scrub meadows.

Your next downhill is a lovely curving descent that turns sharply at the bottom to cross a bridge over a branch of Boston Run. After the climb back up, you can enjoy over 1.5 miles of level to gently rolling terrain. If you are skiing, this is one of the most enjoyable parts of this trail, as you can double-pole at a nice pace through a mature beech forest. Follow the trail along a hemlock ravine, make a hairpin turn to your left, then back into the hardwoods again, coming out along another ravine edge; the creek below flows to the main channel of Boston Run. This is the northernmost point of the trail and the approximate halfway point.

After another 1.3 miles you come to a bench on your right which overlooks a pretty, winding ravine. Just around the bend you find two more benches from which you can view the Boston Run valley. These vantage points are on a plateau between Boston Run and the tributary. On the left are aspen and dogwood trees, indicating an early stage of forest growth. The ravines have mature beeches and maples along the slopes. Below, Boston Run meanders through the fairly wide valley. This is a great spot to sit quietly for a bit of wildlife watching. If you are lucky you may see many birds (especially woodpeckers), small mammals, and perhaps a deer or two.

Follow the trail as it winds along the plateau rim, then descend steeply into the valley of Boston Run one last time. Cross two bridges, then climb very steeply back to the playing field where you began. Turn to the right to return to the parking lot.

Hiking at the Ledges

The Ledges

For many years people have been attracted to the Ritchie Ledges area for its unique natural beauty. The dramatic rock cliffs come as a surprise to someone new to the area. The exposed rock, the graceful hemlocks, the cool water oozing from cracks in the rocks, and the mosses and ferns all seem more like the Canadian north woods. This is understandable, because this habitat we enjoy today is related to the colder climate associated with the glaciers. Some northern species which migrated south before the advancing ice sheets still can be found in these forests. Two common examples are yellow birch trees and eastern hemlocks.

There are three hiking trails in this area, totaling about 5 miles. You can make connections to other trails to lengthen your hike. The scenery, along with many picnic sites, reservable shelters, and large playing field make the Ledges a popular picnicking spot.

The Ledges, Pine Grove, and Forest Point Trails are all part of the Virginia Kendall Unit of Cuyahoga Valley National Recreation Area. This area was Hayward Kendall's country retreat in the early part of the 20th century. Kendall willed 420 acres to the State of Ohio for park purposes and the park was named in memory of his mother. Virginia Kendall Park was managed by the Akron Metropolitan Park District until transfer to the National Park Service in January 1978, when it became the first federal unit of Cuyahoga Valley National Recreation Area.

The Civilian Conservation Corps (CCC) built all the structures in the park in the 1930s. These include the Ledges Shelter, the Octagon Shelter (both reservable), the Lake Shelter, the stone steps to Ice Box Cave, privies, benches, and some roads and trails. The CCC also planted many of the trees and shrubs that you now find along the trails. One of the pleasures of these trails is discovering these reminders of the early days of this park.

The entrance to the Ledges is reached by going south out of Peninsula on Akron Peninsula Road, then east on Truxell Road for about 2.25 miles. You can also reach Truxell Road from Akron Cleveland Road, .75 mile south of State Route 303.

Ledges Trail

The Ledges Trail makes a loop around the Ritchie Ledges, starting out on the top of the rock formation. The ledges are splendid rock outcrops of a formation called Sharon Conglomerate. About 300 million years ago, a large, shallow sea covered this area. The Sharon Conglomerate was formed when fast-moving streams from the north carried sediment into the sea. In time the sediment was compacted into conglomerate rock comprised of cemented sand and small quartz pebbles, rounded and smoothed by the action of the water.

This rock resists erosion and is often found exposed where other materials have eroded away. It usually occurs as the cap rock at 1150 to 1300-feet elevation. That is the case here, where the forces of erosion have sculpted an oval-shaped island of rock. You can also find Sharon Conglomerate rock cliffs at Gorge Metro Park in Cuyahoga Falls, Nelson-Kennedy Ledges in Portage County, and in Jackson County, 150 miles south of here.

A moist, cool microclimate along the ledges encourages the growth of plants which are typical of more northern climes. You can find ferns, starflower, hemlocks (evergreens whose needles are flat with two white lines beneath), and yellow birch trees along the trail. The birches wind their roots over the rock, clinging to whatever they can. Recognize them by their yellowish, peeling bark. The birds you are likely to see include woodpeckers, flycatchers, warblers, wood thrushes, wrens, and more rarely, the brilliantly colored scarlet tanager. They all disappear quickly into the thick woods at your approach, so walk slowly and sit often to enjoy their winged beauty.

Begin the Ledges Trail at the trailhead bulletin board near the Ledges Shelter. Follow the service road north alongside the shelter. All along this road, small trails lead off to picnic tables scattered throughout the woods. At the first true trail intersection, marked with a trail sign, you'll find a wayside illustrating the ledges area. Turn to the right. Soon there is a noticeable change in the woods, from oaks and hickories to hemlocks, and at this point you begin to see the fissured conglomerate.

Follow the trail as it drops alongside the ledges, where you soon reach the oblong-shaped Ledges Trail. You can walk it in either direction—it is described here in a counterclockwise direction. Turn to the left; in about 100 yards is Ice Box Cave. This narrow slit in the rock, not a true cave, reaches 50 feet into the dark dampness. A spring seeps from the rock near a wood bridge just beyond Ice Box Cave. The temperature is noticeably cooler here, and a fern garden thrives on the rock above. Leaving Ice Box Cave, cross the bridge, climb the steps, and continue on. Informal trails to the left lead into the maze of ledges.

Continue on for a quarter of a mile to a bench and a set of stone steps. These steps lead back up to the playing field and picnic area. The Civilian Conservation Corps built the graceful, curving steps out of Berea Sandstone quarried from Deep Lock Quarry. The Ledges Trail continues to follow the base of the ledges. Just beyond the steps you will find a trail to the right which leads to the Haskell Run Trail and Happy Days Visitor Center. Continue around the nose of exposed rock, via boardwalks and steps. You have rounded the northern end of the loop trail. A trail to the left leads back up to the Ledges Shelter, and shortly after this a trail to the right goes to the Octagon Shelter. Stay at the base of the rock if you wish to complete the loop.

Continue along the towering rock face for about .5 mile. The ledges begin to diminish towards the southern point of the loop. At the trail intersection turn to the left and climb the hill. The trail to the right leads to the Lake Shelter, .9 miles away.

When you reach the top of the rock again, watch for side trails leading west towards the edge of the ledges. Follow one of these to find the exposed rock overlook where you can enjoy an expansive view of the Cuyahoga Valley. Past the overlook, bear to the right, skirt the south edge of the field, just inside

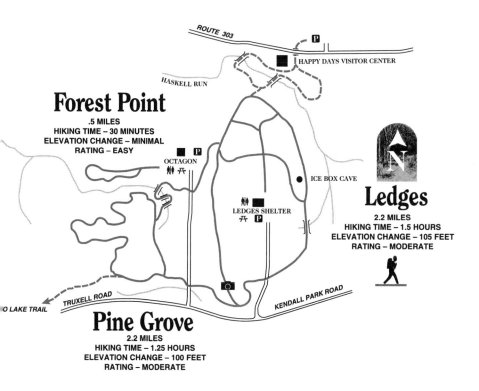

ROUTE 303

HAPPY DAYS VISITOR CENTER

HASKELL RUN

Forest Point
.5 MILES
HIKING TIME – 30 MINUTES
ELEVATION CHANGE – MINIMAL
RATING – EASY

OCTAGON

ICE BOX CAVE

Ledges
2.2 MILES
HIKING TIME – 1.5 HOURS
ELEVATION CHANGE – 105 FEET
RATING – MODERATE

LEDGES SHELTER

O LAKE TRAIL

TRUXELL ROAD

KENDALL PARK ROAD

Pine Grove
2.2 MILES
HIKING TIME – 1.25 HOURS
ELEVATION CHANGE – 100 FEET
RATING – MODERATE

the woods, then cross the entrance drive. After a short walk through deciduous trees, you reach a wooden bridge. Across the bridge is a feathery, fairy-like forest of hemlocks. Complete the loop trail just before Ice Box Cave; watch for the trail leading up to the left to take you to the top of the ledges, then another left that leads back to the shelter. All around the edges of the field, trails lead to picturesque picnic sites where you can get close looks at the cracks and fissures in the rock.

Pine Grove Trail

The Pine Grove Trail circles through the forests west of the Ritchie Ledges in the Virginia Kendall unit of CVNRA. It is named after the pine plantation through which it passes. This trail can be combined with others in the Ledges and Kendall Lake areas for longer hikes. Near the start of the trail is the Octagon Shelter, a Civilian Conservation Corps structure, which is reservable (see Appendix). Picnic sites with grills line the edges of a playing field near the shelter, and restrooms and water are located in Octagon Shelter.

This trail starts from the Octagon Shelter. To reach the shelter, go south of Peninsula on Akron Peninsula Road to Truxell Road and turn left. The entrance drive to the Octagon is about 2 miles down Truxell Road.

Begin Pine Grove Trail at the trailhead bulletin board located at the upper, southeast corner of the Octagon parking lot. The first half mile or so is an access trail to the main loop. Follow this south, crossing the entrance drive, and continue into the woods. You come to a wooden staircase which leads down into a beech and maple ravine. After crossing the creek three times, climb another set of steps to reach the Pine Grove Trail loop.

From here, the Pine Grove Trail can be followed in either direction. To follow the trail counterclockwise, turn to the right; the trail heads north along a ravine. Wind along several small ravines until you come to the red pines for which the trail is named. Pines were often planted in plantations such as this during the reforestation efforts of the 1930s.

Past the pines and about 1 mile from the start of the trail, you come to a trail leading to the right towards Camp Butler. Follow Pine Grove beyond this intersection; it drops part way into a beech ravine, then leaves the beeches to reenter pines. Here you find both red pines (needles two to a bundle and bark reddish) and native white pines (our only pine with five needles to a bundle).

About 3/4 of the way around the loop a trail from the Kendall Lake area comes in from the right. Continuing on around, at the next trail intersection bear to the left; the trail straight ahead leads up to the south end of Ritchie Ledges and the ledges overlook.

An aspen grove borders the pine woods along this portion of the trail. Aspens do well on cut-over areas and probably established themselves here after the area was left to reforest. Soon you have completed the loop; take the trail to the right back across the creek and up the stairs to return to the Octagon Trailhead.

Forest Point Trail

This short, easy trail begins at the southwest corner of the playing field behind the Octagon Shelter. It provides a pleasant walk for people of all ages—perfect for after a holiday picnic!

To reach Octagon Shelter, go south of Peninsula on Akron Peninsula Road to Truxell Road and turn left. The entrance drive to Octagon Shelter is about 2 miles down Truxell Road.

Little description is needed for following the trail. Shortly after entering the woods, the trail splits to the right and left. Follow it in either direction to go out to a point of land overlooking Ritchie Run.

The forest here is typical of deciduous woods of Cuyahoga Valley National Recreation Area. One of the more interesting trees is the beech. The smooth, light gray bark of these large trees makes them stand out from the rest. Beechnuts are a favorite food of wild turkeys which are again inhabiting the valley.

Another tree you see here is the white oak. Its bark is light gray and broken into irregular scales. A white oak can reach a height of 95 feet and is slow growing, living as long as 600 years! The oaks supply plenty of acorns for wildlife and depend on squirrels for propagation: the squirrels bury the acorns as a food cache, some of which sprout as young oaks.

Follow the path back to the field to complete your Forest Point walk.

Kendall Lake Bathhouse & Dock c.1938

Kendall Lake

Kendall Lake is located in the Virginia Kendall Unit of Cuyahoga Valley National Recreation Area. The lake and surrounding hills act like a magnet to fishermen, hikers, and kite flyers from spring through fall and draw skiers, sledders, and snowmen makers in the winter. There is challenging hiking and skiing here and plenty of wide open spaces. Over 8 miles of trails lead into a variety of habitats: woodlands, hemlock ravines, fields, and wetlands. The Kendall Hills, above the lake, offer an excellent vantage point for enjoying autumn's color show.

The Kendall Lake area is part of what was formerly Virginia Kendall Metropolitan Park. In the early part of the 20th century Hayward Kendall, a wealthy Clevelander, owned these acres of forest and farmland and made them his country retreat. Kendall died in 1929, willing his land to be used for public park purposes. His will gave the first option to the National Park Service, which declined it, but the State of Ohio accepted the gift and the Akron Metropolitan Park District agreed to manage the park land. Later, in 1940, the State provided $75,000 for more acreage to be added to Kendall's 420 acres. The park was named Virginia Kendall, in memory of Kendall's mother.

The Civilian Conservation Corps (CCC) accomplished much of the early work of transforming the private retreat into a public park. Structures in the park built by the CCC in the 1930s include Kendall Lake itself, the Lake Shelter (originally used as a swimmers' bathhouse and concession), privies, and toboggan chutes (later removed by the National Park Service due to safety concerns). In 1978, in an ironic turn of history, Virginia Kendall park was transferred to the National Park Service which had declined it in 1929, so that it became the first federal unit of the new Cuyahoga Valley National Recreation Area.

This area is located about 2.5 miles south of Peninsula, on Truxell Road midway between Akron Peninsula Road and Akron Cleveland Road.

Cross Country Trail

The Cross Country Trail was designed for skiing and is equally good for hiking. It winds through the area east of Kendall Lake bounded by Truxell and Quick Roads. It is mostly in the woods but comes out onto Kendall Hills where there is lots of room to practice downhill runs (and falling). The ski trail is separated from the sledding hills, where you can find hundreds of sledders on a snowy weekend.

Most of this area was farmed at one time, and even now you can see evidence of the fields, wood lots, farm lanes, and pastures. The mixture of woods and fields, hills and streams, supports much wildlife. Keep an eye out for mammals, from tiny meadow voles to white-tailed deer. Beaver have begun to inhabit the lake, joining the fish, frogs, mallards, and Canada geese. Many species of birds reside here due to the diversity of habitats.

You can best reach this trail from the Kendall Lake Shelter off Truxell Road but can also access it from Little Meadow Parking Area on Quick Road, just east of the sledding hills. A combination first aid station and all-season restroom facility is located at the sledding hills. The National Ski Patrol, operating out of the first aid station, patrols the trail during ski season.

The Lake Shelter operates as the Winter Sports Center in January and February, offering information, hot drinks, and recreational programs. There are picnic tables near the shelter and restrooms in the lower level. When hiking this trail during the skiing season, please observe the multi-use trail etiquette: refrain from hiking in the ski tracks and yield to skiers, especially on hills. The Cross Country Trail is described in a clockwise direction from the start of the trail at the Lake Shelter parking lot.

Find the trail at the corner of the Lake Shelter parking lot, just to the left of the trailhead bulletin board, marked with a sign "To Cross Country Trail." Begin to climb up a fairly steep, open slope lined by pine trees. Partway up this slope the Lake Trail crosses at right angles; the Cross Country Trail continues straight up the slope. At the top of this slope the trail narrows to a two-person width and continues to climb more gradually. Pines and hardwoods make up the surrounding woods. Sweetgum trees, with their star-shaped leaves, are particularly attractive here in the autumn when the leaves turn yellow and orange on their way to a rich wine color. In pioneer days the resin from these trees was used medicinally and for chewing gum. To the right of the trail is a stand of tulip trees recognized by their tall, straight trunks and tulip-shaped leaves.

In about three-quarters of a mile you reach the location of a former farmstead. A large old white oak towers near the site of the farmhouse and barn. You can still find remains of old foundations in this area, marked by clusters of daffodils in the spring.

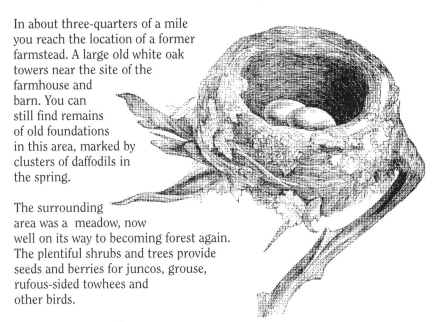

The surrounding area was a meadow, now well on its way to becoming forest again. The plentiful shrubs and trees provide seeds and berries for juncos, grouse, rufous-sided towhees and other birds.

The trail curves and dips slightly to cross a tributary of Salt Run, the creek which feeds Kendall Lake. You then come to where the trail emerges from the woods and continues straight ahead bordered by a mature woods on the left and a meadow on the right. Follow this until the trail veers to the right to cross the meadow. The trail that continues straight leads to Buckeye Sports Center on Akron Cleveland Road. Bear to the right to stay on the Cross Country Trail. Your meadow crossing may be quick, as it can be hot in summer and bitter cold in winter! Its loveliest time is autumn, when goldenrods spread out in all directions.

At the far end of the meadow, reenter the woods and fairly soon begin the steep descent to Salt Run, crossing the creek on a bridge. This narrow descent can be tricky on skis and a strong snowplow maneuver and caution are urged so that you do not miss the bridge! The trail then uses an old roadbed to climb out of the creek valley.

At the top of this hill, make a hairpin turn to the right (a service road straight ahead goes to Quick Road). Now once again high on a plateau, you pass through young forests that were meadows just a decade ago. Soon the trail splits at a "Y" intersection. The branch to the left leads down a hill, across a stream, then up and across a field to Little Meadow Parking Area. The branch to the right is the continuation of the Cross Country Trail. Following it, you soon reach the top of the Kendall Hills. From here you get a good view of the lake shining in the distance at the foot of the hills. Follow your instincts here—run, roll, plow, or plod down the hill in whatever way works best, aiming generally for the lake.

As you approach the lake, the trail intersects with the Lake Trail. Turn to the right to drop down and across Salt Run via a boardwalk. You can take the Lake Trail to the left to circle the lake, but this is suitable for skiing only partway. On the Cross Country Trail, you come to some graceful hemlock trees edging the lake just as you climb a hill to get around a small cove. At the top of the hill, go through a tunnel that was constructed to go under toboggan chutes. The 60-year old chutes deteriorated and were removed in 1990.

After the tunnel, go straight ahead to rejoin the loop on the slope near where you started. A turn to the left takes you back to the parking lot.

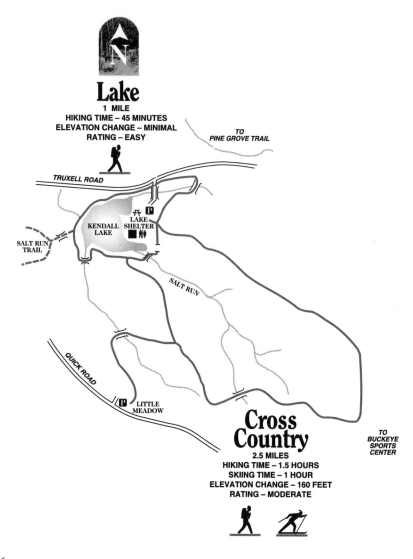

Lake
1 MILE
HIKING TIME – 45 MINUTES
ELEVATION CHANGE – MINIMAL
RATING – EASY

TO
PINE GROVE TRAIL

TRUXELL ROAD

KENDALL LAKE
LAKE SHELTER

SALT RUN TRAIL

SALT RUN

QUICK ROAD

LITTLE MEADOW

Cross Country
2.5 MILES
HIKING TIME – 1.5 HOURS
SKIING TIME – 1 HOUR
ELEVATION CHANGE – 160 FEET
RATING – MODERATE

TO
BUCKEYE
SPORTS
CENTER

Lake Trail

The Lake Trail allows you close access to the entire circumference of Kendall Lake, beautiful in any season. The fairly level trail is suitable for a family stroll and offers good chances to see wildlife. Forest, stream, and lake meet here, providing a rich area for wild plant and animal life to flourish. The most common inhabitants found here are Canada geese, and they share the lake and shores with many other bird species, insects, amphibians, and mammals. You might even see signs of beaver, as they have returned to the valley and have taken up residence in and near the lake.

The Lake Shelter overlooks Kendall Lake. In January and February the shelter serves as a Winter Sports Center offering information, hot drinks, and a place to warm up. In other seasons, the shelter is available on a first-come, first-served basis. The upper and lower porches are particularly nice for picnics, with the lake view framed by the shelter's stone walls. There are other picnic tables and benches on the lawn along the lake. Restrooms are located in the lower level of the shelter. Fishing is permitted in the lake in the summertime, and the small pier is a good place for teaching children the fine art of placing the worm on the hook.

The Lake Trail leaves from the Kendall Lake parking lot off Truxell Road. Reach Truxell Road by going 1 mile south out of Peninsula on Akron Peninsula Road or 1 mile south of State Route 303 on Akron Cleveland Road. The entrance to Kendall Lake is about midway between Akron Peninsula and Akron Cleveland Roads on Truxell Road.

Start the Lake Trail along with the Cross Country Trail; both leave from the southeast corner of the parking lot, near the trailhead bulletin board. Begin to climb the open slope, then turn to the right at the trail intersection to pass through a tunnel. The trail drops down along a cove of the lake then crosses Salt Run on a boardwalk. Shortly after this, the Cross Country Trail goes to the left; to stay on the Lake Trail, continue ahead along the shores of the lake. The trail winds through a narrow band of trees, bordered by the lake to your right and the Kendall Hills to your left. One of the most conspicuous trees is the American hornbeam, a good example of how confusing common names can be. Its sinewy, gray branches resemble muscles, suggesting one common name, muscle wood. It is a member of the birch family, but is also called water beech because it prefers moist soil and the bark resembles that of beech!

As you circle the lake, the view keeps changing. The small, quiet coves are favorite spots for birds, and you may see the smaller of our common herons, the green heron. Beavers have been active here, especially on a small point of land along the cove. About halfway around, cross the earthen dam which forms Kendall Lake from the waters of Salt Run. (At the south end of the dam a trail to the left connects to the Salt Run Trail.) At the north end of the dam, follow the Lake Trail to the right and climb a set of steps to the hill above the shoreline. Mature beech trees frame the Lake Shelter in the distance. Rattlesnake weed, identified by its striking purple-veined leaves, can be found clinging to these slopes, along with club mosses. The club mosses are notable as they are one of the most ancient plants on earth, dating back at least 400 million years.

Descend a short way, climb again, then descend steps to reach the backwaters of the lake. Here is one of the places along the shore where you might be able to spot signs of beaver activity such as sharply pointed, gnawed stumps of saplings. Continue across the Kendall Lake entrance drive. Across Truxell Road, opposite the entrance drive, a connector leads to Pine Grove Trail and access to the Ledges area. The Lake Trail enters a swamp east of the entrance road. Perched on the cattails and tree stumps, red-winged blackbirds and woodpeckers claim their territories. Sounds announce the seasons, with spring peepers proclaiming the return of spring and the dry rustle of cattails ushering in winter.

Leave the swamp by crossing the creek on a bridge, then climb steps into a planted pine forest. Rejoin the Cross Country Trail on the open slope where you began. Turn to the right to reach the parking lot.

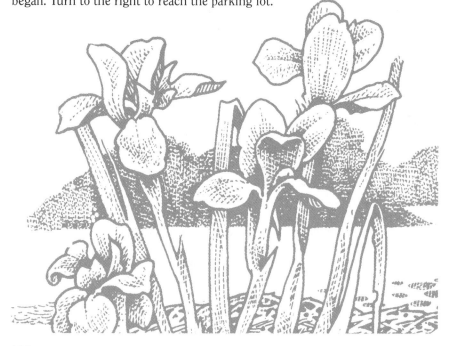

Salt Run Trail

Salt Run Trail, west of Kendall Lake, takes a long route through the forested, rugged hills drained by Salt Run. The length and terrain make this trail more challenging than others in the area, and it can be combined with the Lake and Cross Country Trails for an even longer hike. The short-cut loop on the Salt Run Trail offers a less challenging alternative hike. Both the long and short routes take you through pine, oak, hickory, beech, and hemlock stands. A variety of ferns, including the evergreen Christmas fern, and wildflowers border the trail.

You can reach the Salt Run Trail by taking the Lake Trail from the Kendall Lake parking lot. Kendall Lake is located on Truxell Road, midway between Akron Peninsula Road and Akron Cleveland Road. You can also reach the Salt Run Trail from Pine Hollow parking area at Kendall Hills on Quick Road. Quick Road is 1.4 miles south of Peninsula and runs between Akron Peninsula and State Roads. There are picnic tables, grills, water, and restrooms at both Kendall Lake and Pine Hollow.

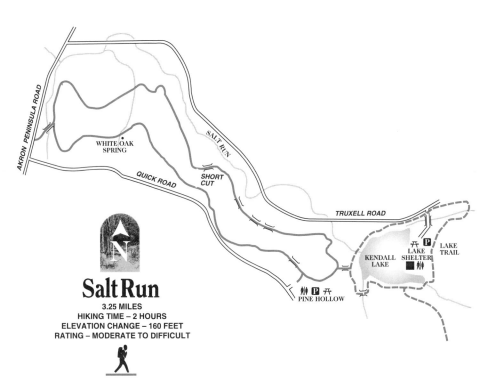

Salt Run

3.25 MILES
HIKING TIME – 2 HOURS
ELEVATION CHANGE – 160 FEET
RATING – MODERATE TO DIFFICULT

To reach the trail from Kendall Lake, follow the Lake Trail south to the far side of the lake; watch for the trail sign at the south end of the dam. Turn away from the lake and follow the trail a short distance to the sign marking the beginning of the 3.25-mile Salt Run Trail. (Here we describe the trail in a clockwise direction.) Go straight ahead, across the bottom of the sledding hills, and into the pine woods. Climb a short distance through the pines; you'll reach another trail sign that marks the trail for those entering from the Pine Hollow parking area on Quick Road.

Bear to the right and descend to cross a stream on a small bridge. Climbing out of this creek valley, continue through a mixed forest for less than .25 mile, then out onto Quick Road in order to get around the head of a narrow ravine. Walk along the road for 70 yards, then follow the trail back into the woods.

About 1 mile from the start, you reach the short-cut trail. Follow this to your right for a shorter loop (shortening the trail by about 1 mile). This area where the short-cut intersects was a clearing in the 1960s. You can still detect the difference between this former clearing and the surrounding forest.

Shortly past the cut-off, you reach a wooden bench overlooking the deciduous forest, then begin a steep drop to the lowlands. A large, old oak tree here in the valley appears to have escaped the saw, and the aging fruit trees nearby now provide food for wildlife. Next is a steady, short climb to White Oak Spring, a natural spring occurring at the base of a white oak tree. Continuing on, you again descend a steep slope to the valley floor. Now near Akron Peninsula Road, the trail follows the route of the older East River Road for a short way. A tributary of Salt Run is on the left, and a side trail (part of the Boy Scout's Order of the Arrow trail) joins in from Akron Peninsula Road.

Just before reaching Salt Run, the trail turns to the right and goes into a thicket of young deciduous trees. These are slowly replacing the scrubby meadow that was here in the 1960s. Being in the lowlands of Salt Run, the trail can be very muddy, but the surrounding wet habitat supports some interesting plants. Mosses, often producing the first green of spring, adorn the rocks and tree trunks. Jewelweed thrives here in the summer along with wild grapes, thistles, goldenrods, thorn apples, and walnut trees. Because of the food and cover, this is a good area for seeing birds and deer. Past this section and on up a narrow ridge, you come to where the short-cut rejoins the main trail.

Past the short-cut, drop down a steep slope then cross a long bridge. You are still in the floodplain of Salt Run. In this creek valley, you come to an area of hemlocks and beeches on an "island" of land separated by drainage cuts in the landscape. Here you can often see remnants of mud slides, exposing clay soils. Many of the slopes in the valley are unstable, and you can find evidence of their movements where slumps like these occur. Cross a side creek via a bridge, follow along the hemlock island, then cross two more bridges placed close together. Some of the evergreen hemlocks here reach heights of 30-50 feet.

Climb up a switchback, leaving the hemlocks behind. You'll reach some white pines mixed in with very tall red and white oaks. Climb some more to reach a white pine grove. A severe storm in 1995 blew down many trees through this area. Follow the trail to the right, then left, and right again, then begin the last climb past some towering oaks. When the leaves are off the trees, you might be able to glimpse Kendall Lake below.

Descend towards the base of the sledding hills to complete the loop. Turn left to return to Kendall Lake, or right to return to the Pine Hollow parking lot.

Deep Lock Quarry in operation

Deep Lock Quarry

Deep Lock Quarry Area contains remains of the valley's quarry, canal, and railroad operations which were active from the mid-nineteenth century to the early twentieth century. The main natural feature is a lovely, fast-flowing stretch of the Cuyahoga River; two main historic features are the Berea Sandstone Quarry and Deep Lock (Lock 28 on the Ohio & Erie Canal). Deep Lock is the deepest lock on the canal and is in good condition. In 1879 Ferdinand Schumacher owned a part of the quarry—he found that the sandstone made good millstones for his American Cereal Works in Akron (later Quaker Oats). You can find discarded millstones along the trails in the quarry area. Stones cut from this quarry also provided building blocks for canal locks and many local structures.

During the heyday of the canal and quarrying era, pioneers stripped this area of its trees. It is now mostly reforested and has one of the finest concentrations of Ohio buckeye trees in the county. The buckeye, Ohio's state tree, is most conspicuous in the spring when it displays 6-inch long, upright flower clusters. In the fall, children (and many adults) enjoy picking up the smooth, brown seed that resembles a buck's eye.

The old canal bed still holds some shallow water. On warm spring days, turtles sun themselves while the croaking of bullfrogs echoes off the lock walls. A shallow marsh at the base of the quarry walls features many plants including the infrequently found narrow-leaved cattail and rose pink. This area is also a popular spot for birders, especially during the spring migration. On a relatively short walk, you might spot flycatchers, a number of different warblers, orioles, vireos, sparrows, finches, and perhaps a thrush or a brilliant scarlet tanager. Along the river you might see great blue herons, geese, kingfishers, and woodpeckers. This is a small area, but with much to see!

Deep Lock Quarry has two hiking trails, the Quarry Trail and the Towpath Trail. Both loop trails overlap each other and could be walked as one trail. The Buckeye Trail (a 1200 mile loop trail) uses the Ohio & Erie Canal Towpath Trail as it passes through Deep Look. It is marked with a blue BT in a directional arrow. Picnic sites and toilets are located near the parking lot.

Reach Deep Lock Quarry from Riverview Road, south of Peninsula. The entrance drive is .75 miles south of State Route 303.

The Towpath Trail in Deep Lock is a short loop trail that incorporates part of the canal towpath, as distinguished from the much longer, 20-mile Ohio & Erie Canal Towpath Trail which is the major north-south spine trail in CVNRA. "Towpath" signifies the path alongside the canal that was used by the mules as they towed the canal boats.

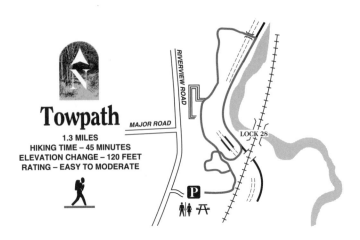

Towpath

MAJOR ROAD

1.3 MILES
HIKING TIME – 45 MINUTES
ELEVATION CHANGE – 120 FEET
RATING – EASY TO MODERATE

In Deep Lock Quarry, start the Towpath Trail from the north edge of the parking lot. From the parking lot, follow the wide trail down towards the railroad tracks used by the Cuyahoga Valley Scenic Railroad. The trail levels off and is bordered by scattered millstones and small mounds from the quarrying days when workers scraped soil off the underlying sandstone to expose it for cutting.

At the trail juncture, follow the Towpath Trail to the right, descending to the canal bed and Deep Lock. Lock 28 is 17 feet deep (locks were usually no more than 12 to 14 feet deep); all the workings of the lock are gone now, however, iron guides for the balance beams that opened and closed the main gate remain at each end of the lock.

The southern end of the lock is dry; cross here to the other side. At this point the Towpath Trail joins the longer, multi-use Ohio & Erie Canal Towpath Trail and the Buckeye Trail. Partially visible off to the right is the remains of another sandstone structure, the canal's spillway, which carried excess water around the canal structures. Turn left and follow the Towpath Trail along the edge of the lock then descend to parallel the Cuyahoga River.

Along the Cuyahoga

At the next trail junction, the Buckeye Trail goes straight north towards Peninsula, staying on the longer Towpath Trail, while this Towpath loop trail (for hikers only) leaves the multi-use trail and crosses the canal. From here, climb up the hill and join the Quarry Trail. Follow both trails to the left, along a ridge above the river.

Along this path you can still find pieces of the old railroad siding leading into the quarry. The trail now follows the old railroad bed, turning away from the river and into the base of the quarry itself.

After exploring the quarry, leave the area via the Towpath Trail on a wide path heading south. (The Quarry Trail goes in the opposite direction, climbing up and around the top of the quarry). At the next junction, turn to the right and go up a small hill past other old quarry-related foundations. Follow the trail around and then rejoin the main trail just at the foot of the hill. Turn right to climb back to the parking lot.

Quarry Trail

The Quarry Trail makes a loop through the remains of the Berea Sandstone quarry that furnished much of the stone for local foundations, millstones, and canal locks.

Begin this trail along with the Towpath Trail, from the Deep Lock parking lot. Descend the hill and follow the trail straight ahead. At the trail junction, continue straight on the Quarry Trail towards the quarry; the Towpath Trail, branching to the right, leads to Deep Lock. Once at the quarry, step with caution as the stones are often wet and slippery.

The quarry provided sandstone for many regional structures including the first section of Akron City Hospital. The stone was also used in building the breakwall in Cleveland, along with the intake crib in Lake Erie where Cleveland's water supply inlet is located. After 1879, Ferdinand Schumacher began using the stones as hulling stones at his American Cereal Works in Akron (later to become Quaker Oats). Schumacher is credited with introducing oatmeal to America, so these stones deserve a place of honor in America's breakfast history!

Early quarrying was slow, difficult work performed with hand tools. Workers risked their health as they faced occupational hazards, including lung damage from inhaling the fine stone grit. Small sponges tied under the noses of quarry workers were the precursors of today's masks. Late in the 1880s, the introduction of mechanization altered the quarrying process. One of the new machines was a channeling machine driven by a steam engine. It traveled on a portable track, driving bits against the stone, cutting a channel about three inches wide. By cutting such channels at right angles, the stone could be "cubed," and the bottom side loosened by wedges or a small blast. You can still see the channel marks in the remaining, exposed sandstone of the quarry.

After exploring the quarry bottom, leave via the Quarry Trail by turning to the right of the sandstone walls. Follow the sign to the quarry rim, climbing the hill via some steep steps. From the rim, you gain a full view of the quarry area. Please be careful while exploring around the steep-walled quarry. Now follow the Quarry Trail away from the rim; it bears to the right and soon joins the Towpath Trail. Both trails turn south to reenter the quarry along the route of an old railroad spur. Exit the quarry the way you came in, going south on the wide trail. At the next junction, turn to the right and go up a small hill past other old quarry-related foundations. Follow this short section until it rejoins the main trail just at the foot of the first hill. Turn right to climb the hill to the parking lot.

Quarry

1.2 MILES
HIKING TIME – 40 MINUTES
ELEVATION CHANGE – 120 FEET
RATING – EASY TO MODERATE

Millstones

The Gilson Family

Oak Hill

This upland plateau contains one of the largest roadless areas of contiguous federally owned land in the recreation area. The area is dotted by numerous small ponds and contains stands of mature oak and hickory trees, plus meadows, pine plantations, and a former Christmas tree farm. The Oak Hill and Horseshoe Pond Trailheads serve the area. There are picnic tables at Oak Hill and picnic tables under a pavilion at Horseshoe Pond; neither area has running water, but both have portable toilets.

The Cuyahoga Valley Environmental Education Center is adjacent to the Oak Hill Day Use Area. The center is operated by the National Park Service and the Cuyahoga Valley Association, offering programs year-round to area school children and adults. The use of the campus areas is reserved for groups using the center (see Appendix); these reserved areas are posted. Classes may also be using the Oak Hill trails—should you encounter a class in session, please be considerate and do not interrupt.

Much of the Oak Hill area was farmed in earlier times. One of the oldest farmhouses in the vicinity, the Gilson home, now serves as a dormitory for the environmental education center, while the handsome barn has a new use housing a dining hall and laboratory classroom. In 1877, Mr. Gilson lost his life in attempting to cross Furnace Run during high water; in his memory the local residents pressed to have the Everett Road Covered Bridge erected to provide safe crossing. Damaged by a careless truck driver, then destroyed by a flood in 1975, it was rebuilt by the park service and reopened to non-motorized traffic in 1986.

Fishing in the three small ponds behind the environmental education center is "reserved for wildlife," however, fishermen can try their luck at one of four other public ponds in the Oak Hill area — Meadowedge, Sylvan, Goosefeather, or Horseshoe.

There are three different hiking trails here: Oak Hill Trail and Plateau Trail in the Oak Hill Day Use Area, and the Tree Farm Trail in the Horseshoe Pond Area. Plateau Trail and Tree Farm Trail are both designed especially for cross-country skiing, and the Oak Hill Trail is also skiable. Tree Farm Trail crosses gently rolling terrain and is a good trail for beginning skiers. Both Oak Hill and Plateau Trails have steeper hills and more challenging turns.

Tree Farm Trail

Tree Farm Trail traverses what was part of the Robert Bishop family Christmas tree farm. This was a "cut your own" tree farm. In December, cars would line Major Road as each family hunted for their special Christmas tree. The Bishops have roots far back into Peninsula history, and Robert Bishop's daughter and son-in-law continue family tradition by operating a tree farm on part of the original acreage. Although the Tree Farm Trail is entirely on public land, it approaches near to the Bishop's private property. Please respect these property lines when exploring this lovely trail.

The topography here is gently rolling and the ski trail is wide with generally good sight lines, making this an excellent novice to intermediate level trail. Some second growth hardwoods and large open fields with good views of the valley interrupt the broad stands of evergreens. Snow-laden evergreen tunnels add to the appeal of this trail. Though bordered by two roads and the village of Peninsula, you will usually find the trail conveys a feeling of quiet and remoteness.

Wildlife is abundant here due to diversity of shelter and food. It is possible to see deer, fox, and coyote. This is also excellent bird habitat, and a keen eye may spot several species of warblers, yellow-breasted chats, cedar waxwings, cardinals, hawks, field sparrows, and perhaps an owl.

Tree Farm Trail is located on Major Road off Riverview Road, .5 mile south of Peninsula. From Riverview Road, it is .8 mile to the trailhead, marked as Horseshoe Pond. Horseshoe Pond is a popular fishing pond, where lucky anglers catch bass or bluegill. There is a small parking lot here. From the parking lot, a short trail leads around the pond to the left, reaching a picnic pavilion with a pleasant view of the pond. This trail incorporates a fishing pier, a casting platform, and a boardwalk. Volunteers with the Cuyahoga Valley Trails Council partnered with the National Park Service to fund and build these improvements. Other funds came from the Cuyahoga Valley Association's March for Parks, the Telephone Pioneers of America, and the National Park Foundation. Tree Farm Trail begins from the parking area, to the right of the pond, and is a loop trail. It is described here in a clockwise direction to get the best views.

Tree Farm Trail begins at the trail sign located adjacent to the paved path from the parking lot. Take the left fork to the earthen dam of Horseshoe Pond, then across the dam itself. At the end of the dam, watch for the trail sign indicating a turn into the woods to the right. This begins a gently rolling and curving section of trail that uses some of the old tree farm lanes.

Tree Farm

2.75 MILES
HIKING TIME – 1.5 HOURS
SKIING TIME – 45 MINUTES
ELEVATION CHANGE – 80 FEET
RATING – EASY TO MODERATE

VILLAGE OF
PENINSULA

WOODRIDGE INTERMEDIATE
SCHOOL

HORSESHOE POND

MAJOR ROAD

RIVERVIEW ROAD

After about one-half mile, you come into a more open area where brambles and multiflora rose repel hikers and entice birds. Soon after, the trail passes through an evergreen tunnel then breaks out into an open field. Follow the path to the top of the open knoll at an elevation of 890 feet; here you can see across the valley to the east. The high points on the opposite rim are at the Ledges Area. Closer by and just below, you can see the neatly planted rows of evergreens at the tree farm.

Descend the hill and cross a former farm lane lined with trees. Continue on through a young woods, then drop down a small hill to cross a stream via a bridge. A bench further along the way is a good spot to sit and watch for deer.

You are about half-way around the trail and fairly close to Riverview Road at this point. The latter half of the trail continues a winding course through evergreens and along sumac and dogwood shrub thickets. You are paralleling Riverview Road, then Major Road. Follow the trail as it curves away from Major Road, then in and out of evergreens again, using the farm lanes.

Near the end of the trail you come out of one of these lanes towards an open field; turn sharply to the right. Descend this slope and turn left to go back into the evergreens. Come out into the open again, bear to the right and cross a small intermittent steam via a bridge. Horseshoe Pond is ahead and to the right, and in a few yards you reach the parking lot where you began.

Oak Hill Trail

The National Park Service opened the Oak Hill Day Use Area in 1983. It offers a small picnic area, fishing, hiking, and cross-country skiing. The western part of this area was farmed in the past and is now meadowy; the eastern section is forested. Historically, this woods was primarily a mixed oak-chestnut forest. Early in the 20th century, chestnut blight, an introduced fungal disease, spread into Ohio and killed most of the American chestnut trees. Bare snags of the chestnuts endure throughout the woods, a testament to the loss of a beautiful species. Young chestnuts continue to sprout and live a few years. Researchers continue to try to find a strain of chestnut that can survive the blight.

The Oak Hill Trail is designed for easy hiking or cross-country skiing and provides access to two of the more remote fishing ponds in the recreation area. It can be quite muddy in places—hiking boots are recommended. There are several stream crossings, all on bridges or boardwalks.

A Youth Conservation Corps crew cleared this trail originally, then when the Cuyahoga Valley Trails Council was established, the council adopted this trail and has made many improvements including installing bridges, a boardwalk, and turnpiking, all aimed at keeping you from getting too mired in the mud. The National Park Service has rebuilt the dams on two ponds in the area plus a third, Goosefeather, located just north of Oak Hill at Scobie Road. All these ponds are good for fishing and ideal for introducing young people to the beauty and delight of pond life.

The Oak Hill Day Use Area is south of Peninsula. From Riverview Road turn west onto Major Road. From Major Road, turn onto Oak Hill Road. The entrance drive to the area is 1 mile south on Oak Hill Road.

The loop trail starts from the eastern edge of the parking lot at the trailhead bulletin board. About a half mile walk in either direction will bring you to Sylvan Pond. From the Oak Hill Trail you can also reach Meadowedge Pond via a portion of the Plateau Trail.

Leaving from the information bulletin board and taking the trail to the right, in a counterclockwise direction, start out along a former farm field. Since the field is no longer used for agriculture, it is naturally revegetating in a process called succession. Right now there are mostly grasses, wildflowers, and shrubs, such as grey dogwood, providing habitat for butterflies, birds, small mammals, and many other creatures. If natural changes are allowed to continue, the grasses and shrubs will eventually be replaced by woodland.

Some of the plants you may find in this and other meadows are wild strawberries and cinquefoil in the spring, followed by the colorful mix of Queen Anne's lace, goldenrod, and ironweed in the late summer and fall. Huge ant hills dot the field, and other insects such as grasshoppers and praying mantises find plentiful shelter and food throughout the varied plants.

Continuing on the trail, you reach a young forest of oaks and hawthorns, cross a small stream via a bridge, then come to a trail intersection. Here the Plateau Trail joins from the right and continues with the Oak Hill Trail for the next section. Both trails bear to the left and pass through a young woods; a meadow and the Cuyahoga Valley Environmental Education Center campuses are to the right. Continue through an area bordered by hawthorns and black cherries until you reach the next trail junction. The Oak Hill Trail turns to the left; a side trip on the Plateau Trail to the right leads to Meadowedge Pond. This little pond is typical of man-made farm ponds. It is a lovely spot any time of year. In the warm months, you can listen to harrumphs of bullfrogs calling from the lily pads and the chickaree of red-winged blackbirds in the cattails. Follow the same trail to return to the Oak Hill Trail.

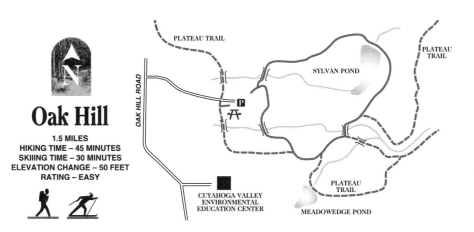

Oak Hill

1.5 MILES
HIKING TIME – 45 MINUTES
SKIIING TIME – 30 MINUTES
ELEVATION CHANGE – 50 FEET
RATING – EASY

PLATEAU TRAIL

PLATEAU TRAIL

SYLVAN POND

OAK HILL ROAD

CUYAHOGA VALLEY
ENVIRONMENTAL
EDUCATION CENTER

PLATEAU TRAIL

MEADOWEDGE POND

The Oak Hill Trail continues through the woods then descends to cross the same creek you crossed earlier. The Plateau Trail joins the Oak Hill Trail to cross this bridge then leaves again. Now the Oak Hill Trail enters an older oak/hickory/maple woods and climbs very gently to the highest point along the trail, a small pine-forested knoll. Leaving the pines, bear to the left and go towards Sylvan Pond, about twice the size of Meadowedge Pond. The trail passes the pond on the pond's dam then reenters the woods at the far end. A short walk of 10 to 15 minutes takes you through a young mixed woods and back to the parking lot.

Plateau Trail

This 4.5 mile loop trail around the Oak Hill plateau was planned and graded as a cross-country ski trail. It traverses one of the largest roadless areas in the recreation area. The Oak Hill Trail is a smaller 1.5 mile loop trail within the larger Plateau Trail and together they can be used to create trips of different lengths.

The Oak Hill Day Use Area is south of Peninsula. From Riverview Road turn west onto Major Road. From Major Road, turn onto Oak Hill Road. The entrance drive to the area is 1 mile south on Oak Hill Road.

Please note: the northern section of the Plateau Trail is anticipated to be completed in the fall of 1997. The description that follows may vary slightly from the finished trail.

This hiking/skiing trail begins at the lone shagbark hickory tree which shades the picnic tables south of the parking area. The trail starts with a short walk through the field west of the picnic area. The loop trail begins just after you enter a spruce plantation beyond the field. The trail is described in a counterclockwise direction. Head south (left), crossing some small headwater drainages. The trail swings east, through a stand of young red maples, then continues through a young beech-maple woods. One-half mile from the start of the trail you join the Oak Hill Trail, skirting a meadow and following an old lane lined with hawthorns and black cherries. The Plateau Trail then leaves the Oak Hill Trail, turning south (right) toward Meadowedge Pond. At the pond, turn left and cross the dam of the pond. You may notice signs at each end of the pond telling you about the Cuyahoga Valley Environmental Education Center. The center is reserved for students or others who are staying on campus; please do not enter without permission. For more information, see the Appendix.

After crossing the dam, turn left and enter the woods. Nearly one-half mile from Meadowedge Pond a spur trail leaves to the right—this trail, used by the environmental education center, parallels a beautiful hemlock ravine and leads to a scenic "study area." Return by the same trail. On the main trail you cross a bridge just before the Plateau Trail joins the Oak Hill Trail again. Soon the Plateau Trail leaves the Oak Hill Trail to the right—this time for good—and provides an opportunity to observe the hemlock ravine from the opposite side of the creek. Take a moment to walk to the edge of the ravine and observe how it rapidly increases in width and depth, a dramatic example of the forces of erosion from water, wind, and ice.

The trail then bears northeast, crosses a bridge, then goes northwest as you circle the oak populated knoll that gave the area its name. You then reach a stand of pines. Here you cross the remains of an old driveway.

154

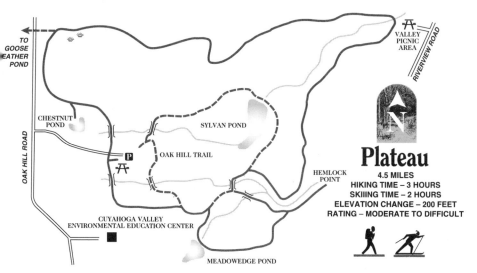

TO GOOSE FEATHER POND

VALLEY PICNIC AREA

RIVERVIEW ROAD

CHESTNUT POND

SYLVAN POND

OAK HILL ROAD

OAK HILL TRAIL

HEMLOCK POINT

N

Plateau

4.5 MILES
HIKING TIME – 3 HOURS
SKIIING TIME – 2 HOURS
ELEVATION CHANGE – 200 FEET
RATING – MODERATE TO DIFFICULT

CUYAHOGA VALLEY
ENVIRONMENTAL EDUCATION CENTER

MEADOWEDGE POND

(Sylvan Pond can be reached by following the drive to the left.) The trail continues through a thick conifer plantation before breaking out onto a plateau with a ravine to your left. The trail winds down a long gently sloping tongue of land before making a sharp turn to the west (left). If you are on skis, enjoy this wonderful downhill run, but remember what goes down, must come up! Here the trail joins another lane. If you take the lane to the right, you will reach the Valley Picnic Area on Riverview Road (with picnic tables and toilets, but no drinking water). The Plateau Trail turns west (left) for the steady climb back up to the plateau.

Once back on the high ground, you swing north then west as the trail winds through the forest. In the woods you will find large trees in a row between younger even-aged woods. These mark old fence lines separating farm fields. As the trail crosses a bridge, note the depth of the ravine here and compare it to the depth just a short distance downstream. After a short traverse across the corner of a field, you enter another tree line and follow along another, shallower ravine.

Soon you pass a small pond before the last leg of the trail turns south. Here, if you head west and cross Oak Hill Road, a grassy access lane will lead you to Goosefeather Pond, a side trip not to be missed by pond aficionados. A little further on the main trail a side trail leads to Chestnut Pond. Although not deep enough to be developed for fishing (by humans), Chestnut Pond provides habitat and shelter to wetland flora and fauna. Through the natural process of eutrafication, the pond will turn into wet meadow, which eventually will turn into forest.

Continue south and cross one last bridge as you enter a spruce plantation then cross the entrance road. You reach the end of the loop; turn left to return to the parking lot.

155

Park Visitors in Horse and Buggy

Wetmore & Riding Run Bridle Trails

The Wetmore Trailhead is the starting place for eight interconnected trails designed primarily for horseback riding. The five trails in the Wetmore area, located on the east side of the Cuyahoga River, cross the wooded ridges and stream bottoms of Dickerson Run and Langes Run, through acreage once used for raising horses. Scattered throughout the area are old barns, shelters, and horse pastures, all reminders of the earlier farming days. Across the valley, on the western side of the river, the Riding Run area offers two trails, Riding Run Trail and Perkins Trail. The Valley Trail links the two clusters of trails. All these trails can also be accessed from the Everett Road Covered Bridge Trailhead on Everett Road, west of Riverview Road. Selecting different combinations allows you to plan rides from 1 mile to 16 miles or more.

The name Wetmore dates back to Frederick and Emila Wetmore, landowners here in the late 1800s. Several owners have succeeded them, the most recent private landowner being a nationally recognized breeder of Morgan and thoroughbred horses. Some of this land was acquired by Metro Parks, Serving Summit County, then in 1984 the National Park Service purchased the remainder of the farms. The current Wetmore trails follow old logging roads and horse paths used by previous owners.

The Riding Run and Perkins Trails travel through wooded hills above the Furnace Run valley. Most of the land was acquired by Metro Parks, Serving Summit County, in the 1970s. The trails make use of some former roads and drives as well as paths used in the past for horseback riding. Both trails cross federal land as well, and the Perkins Trail briefly enters a corner of Hale Farm and Village property.

Much of the trail routing and clearing of the bridle trails was accomplished by volunteers from the Ohio Valley Trail Riders (the Medina County Chapter of the Ohio Horseman's Council) in cooperation with the National Park Service. The Ohio Valley Trail Riders continue to maintain the trails in partnership with the National Park Service trail crew.

At the time of this writing, plans are underway to extend the Valley Trail to connect these southern trails to the bridle trails of Cleveland Metroparks' Brecksville and Bedford Reservations in the north half of the valley.

Wetmore Trail

Situated entirely between Wetmore and Quick Roads, Wetmore Trail's 4 miles goes through most of the area drained by Dickerson Run. Ironically the trail name, which comes from an earlier landowner in the area, also aptly describes the trail's condition: the bottom lands here can be very muddy, especially in the spring! However, besides the wetness you'll find clear running creeks, deep woods, wildflowers, and acres of solitude.

To reach the Wetmore Trailhead, travel south out of Peninsula on Akron Peninsula Road. Wetmore Road is the third road to the left, 1.75 miles from Peninsula. The parking lot, located one-half mile up the road, has ample space for horse trailers. A picnic table and picket lines are there for your use, but no potable water.

Wetmore Trail starts at the trailhead bulletin board at the east end of the Wetmore Trailhead parking lot. From the bulletin board, follow the trail down along the fenced pastures and into a mixed woods of aspens, red maples, and sycamores. In about a quarter mile you will come to the sign indicating the start of the Wetmore Trail loop—take the circular trail in either direction at this point. Our description will follow the trail to the right (counterclockwise).

Here in the lowlands the trail crosses bridges over tributaries of Dickerson Run and passes fields that were formerly pastures. It can be very muddy in this section. Follow the fence line until you reach the intersection with the Dickerson Run Trail. Here the Wetmore Trail turns uphill, away from the creek, and enters a forested area. At the top of this ridge you find fairly level ground for about 1 mile. Even this high ground can be quite muddy where it is not well drained. Dickerson Run valley is off to your right but well out of sight.

Along this high ground, you come to the intersection with Dickerson Run Trail coming in on your right, then Tabletop Trail going off to the left. Continue on Wetmore Trail in a generally south to southeast direction. About halfway around the 4-mile loop, you enter an area of planted trees, mostly white and red pines and spruces, then pass over a bridge spanning a tributary, and follow along a large meadow until you reach the other end of Tabletop Trail. Go past this intersection and past a tiny pond which is slowly silting in.

Leaving the meadow and high ground, descend into the bottom lands and cross a bridge. Come out of the creek valley on an uphill stretch of trail, then parallel Quick Road. You are now heading northwest. Grasses, field wildflowers, and young tulip trees favor these sunnier, open sections of the trail.

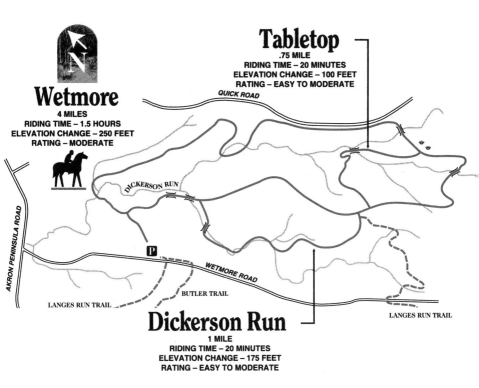

Tabletop

.75 MILE
RIDING TIME – 20 MINUTES
ELEVATION CHANGE – 100 FEET
RATING – EASY TO MODERATE

QUICK ROAD

Wetmore

4 MILES
RIDING TIME – 1.5 HOURS
ELEVATION CHANGE – 250 FEET
RATING – MODERATE

DICKERSON RUN

AKRON PENINSULA ROAD

P

WETMORE ROAD

BUTLER TRAIL

LANGES RUN TRAIL

LANGES RUN TRAIL

Dickerson Run

1 MILE
RIDING TIME – 20 MINUTES
ELEVATION CHANGE – 175 FEET
RATING – EASY TO MODERATE

After paralleling Quick Road for about one-half mile, the trail turns left to drop down to the bottom lands. Follow this down and across a branch of Dickerson Run. Cross a second time, then leave the valley on a relatively steep climb. Large old oak trees dominate the ridge here, and if the branches are bare you can glimpse the meandering course of the stream below.

Soon you reach a switchback down into the stream valley. At the bottom, cross the stream and bear to the right, past a grove of Ohio buckeye trees. This state tree of Ohio can be recognized by its five leaflets forming a single leaf. In early spring, the buckeye's large buds swell and open to reveal inner greenish and rose scales. The five part leaflet emerges fanlike, followed by pale yellow-green flower clusters. Even more familiar to Ohioans, however, is the tree's fruit—a thick, prickly round capsule which breaks open to release the shiny, brown nut resembling a "buck's eye."

Follow the trail on a short climb out of the bottom land and into an old pasture. You might see deer here—watch for the white flag of their tail as they signal alarm. At the signpost, you have completed the 4-mile loop; turn right to climb back up to the parking lot.

Dickerson Run Trail

Dickerson Run Trail, in the Wetmore Bridle Trail system, is only 1 mile, but you must take Wetmore Trail to reach it, so the overall length is at least 2.5 miles. The trail follows Dickerson Run; half of the distance is in the creek valley, the other half on the ridge above the stream.

To reach Dickerson Run Trail, start from the Wetmore Trailhead bulletin board. Follow the trail down to where the Wetmore Trail splits to the right and left (less than one-quarter mile). Turn to the right and go about another one-quarter mile to the intersection of Dickerson Run and Wetmore Trails.

Turn to the right to begin Dickerson Run Trail. For the first half mile or so, the trail stays in the stream lowlands and can be quite muddy. There are rewards, however. Many wildflowers thrive in these wet places, and you can also find several different fern species, including the delicate black stemmed maidenhair fern.

About halfway on Dickerson Run Trail you begin the climb out of the creek valley and onto the ridge. In fall and winter there are some nice views off to the right. Langes Run Trail comes in from the right near the intersection with Wetmore Trail. Climb some more, through planted pines, just before joining the Wetmore Trail. At this point you have several options for returning to the trailhead. Turning to the left on Wetmore Trail is the shortest way back. Longer trips can be made taking Wetmore in the other direction or Langes Run Trail to the southwest.

Tabletop Trail

Tabletop Trail, in the Wetmore Bridle Trail system, is only .75 mile long, but to reach it you must travel 1.5 miles; round trips are about 4.5 miles. This trail follows the high "tabletop" plateau of land between the branches of Dickerson Run and includes a steep descent and climb at its western end.

To reach the start of Tabletop Trail, follow Wetmore Trail from the trailhead bulletin board for one-quarter mile, then turn to the right where Wetmore Trail splits to begin its loop. Go 1.5 miles on Wetmore Trail to reach the start of Tabletop Trail which goes off to the left just past the junction with Dickerson Run Trail.

Tabletop Trail goes through a corridor of white pines, red maples, and flowering dogwoods before entering an oak-hickory forest. The beautiful white blossoms of the dogwoods line this trail in the spring, and in the fall witch hazel closes out the season with its tiny yellow blossoms. All along this trail is an abundant supply of nuts and acorns supplying food for many squirrels and chipmunks. Follow this level tabletop to a switchback down to the stream.

Cross the stream on a wooden bridge, then climb out of the valley through a beech-maple woods. The trail finishes on high ground, rejoining Wetmore Trail at the edge of a pasture. To return to the trailhead, take Wetmore Trail in either direction, about 2 miles either way.

Langes Run Trail

Langes Run Trail in the Wetmore Bridle Trail system includes a bit of every-thing: high meadows, ponds, stream bottom lands, and steep, wooded slopes. To make a loop trip, combine this trail with Dickerson Run and Wetmore Trails (6-9 miles depending on your chosen route).

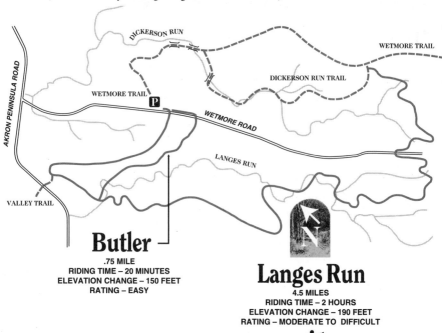

Butler

.75 MILE
RIDING TIME – 20 MINUTES
ELEVATION CHANGE – 150 FEET
RATING – EASY

Langes Run

4.5 MILES
RIDING TIME – 2 HOURS
ELEVATION CHANGE – 190 FEET
RATING – MODERATE TO DIFFICULT

To begin Langes Run Trail, leave the Wetmore Trailhead parking area and cross Wetmore Road. A sign indicates the start of the trail, on an old farm lane. Follow the mowed path around the edge of the pasture. There are two routes through the meadow which soon converge into one trail. From this 870-foot elevation there are good views of the valley to the west. Nestled in the fields are two farm ponds. The fields themselves are full of sun-loving plants.

At the far end of the meadow, the trail begins to descend into the woods. You reach the intersection with the Valley Trail one-half mile from the trailhead, just before ending the descent. At the bottom of the slope follow an old fence line bordering a cultivated field. Akron Peninsula Road can be seen beyond the field. One-half mile further along, and while still down in the lowlands, you come to the intersection with Butler Trail. Continuing on Langes Run Trail, cross Langes Run then climb a hill to an oak-hickory forest.

The trail stays in the woods until coming to a utility right-of-way clearing. Turn left into the right-of-way, then in a short distance, turn right, back into the woods. Next, the trail goes through two meadows in the process of succession. Aspens are pioneer species here, helping revert the meadows to forest. Still on the ridge, you come into a dense woods of maples, ashes, aspens, tulip trees, and sassafras.

Descend once again to the stream valley; you are at the midway point on the trail. The meandering nature of Langes Run is soon evident as you cross it numerous times. This section of the trail can be quite muddy. Leaving the creek valley, the trail begins to switchback up the hillside to reach an oak-hickory forest. Once up on the high ground, take a hard left to use a bridge over a muddy area created by a small frog pond on your right, then follow the trail back down into a creek valley. Cross the creek and climb again, coming out to Wetmore Road. You have completed 3.5 miles of the trail.

Cross Wetmore Road and continue on Langes Run Trail. After crossing a field, the trail turns right, bordering the edge of a ravine, then comes out onto a private driveway. Turn left and follow the driveway for a short distance, then left again into the woods. After the woods you go into a large meadow then descend to a stream. Make a right turn to make the final climb out of this valley and reach the end of Langes Run Trail where it meets Dickerson Run Trail and, in a short distance, Wetmore Trail.

To return to the parking lot by the most direct route, follow the Dickerson Run Trail to the left or go on to the Wetmore Trail and turn left.

Butler Trail

Butler Trail, part of the Wetmore Bridle Trail system, connects Langes Run Trail to Wetmore Road, partially using an old brick road. Reach the trail by following Langes Run Trail through the meadows for 1 mile to where the two trails intersect or by following Wetmore Road southeast (left out of the parking lot) for about one-sixth mile.

Accessing the trail from Langes Run Trail, turn left onto Butler Trail. For about half its length, Butler Trail follows the meanders of Langes Run through a wet bottom land habitat of cottonwood and sycamore trees. Coltsfoot, an early spring wildflower, is abundant in this area.

Cross Langes Run twice, then climb out of the valley on a brick road which was once a connection between Wetmore and Akron Peninsula Roads. Turn left onto Wetmore Road to return to the Wetmore Trailhead.

Valley Trail

Valley Trail connects the Wetmore Bridle Trail system on the east side of the Cuyahoga River valley to Riding Run and Perkins Trails on the west side of the valley. The 2.75 mile Valley Trail goes along the Cuyahoga River, skirting a number of sweet corn fields. Two stream crossings allow for horse watering. The muddiest areas are avoided or eliminated by the use of culverts. The trail is basically flat, with one-quarter mile of road riding and one railroad crossing. In the future, the Valley Trail will be extended to the north following the Cuyahoga River. It will connect all the southern bridle trails with those to the north in Brecksville and Bedford Reservations.

To reach the eastern end of the Valley Trail, follow Langes Run Trail from the Wetmore Trailhead until the trail descends into the woods. Just prior to the end of the descent, a sign for the Valley Trail indicates a right turn toward Akron Peninsula Road.

After crossing Akron Peninsula Road, the trail passes through a grove of aspens and reaches the first stream crossing at Langes Run. Leaving the stream, climb a short hill. The trail passes through a thick patch of blackberries, then begins following the edges of corn fields, with one short stretch following a farm lane. As the trail winds its way towards Bolanz Road along the Cuyahoga River, you can see why the river is also called the "crooked river." In autumn, you'll likely encounter flocks of Canada geese and crows foraging the corn fields. Earlier, yellow and white blossoms line the streambanks. After crossing Robinson Run and following along a corn field you reach a meadowy area lined with sumac shrubs. The handsome home to the east is the historic Point farm, currently housing the Cuyahoga Valley Association and National Park Service offices.

Immediately after going over a three-culvert crossing, bear left into the woods to avoid a very muddy area. After the woods, there is another low area that is consistently wet but safe to ride through. Parallel Akron Peninsula Road, then turn right to follow a tree line for a short ways. Turn left to cross a small gully, then turn right and follow the edge of the field to Bolanz Road (this is private property). Follow Bolanz Road for one-quarter mile, using the road bridge to cross the Cuyahoga River. Turn right just before reaching Hunt Farm, the cluster of white buildings west of the river. A hitching rail for the horses allows you to take some time to explore Hunt Farm Visitor Information Center, fill up on water, or stop at Szalay's Sweet Corn Farm for sweet corn, fresh fruit, or a cool drink.

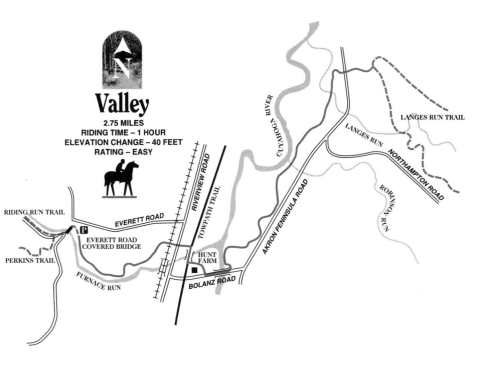

The crossroads hamlet of Everett, which included Hunt and Szalay farms, residences, and various small enterprises, is now recognized as the Everett Historic District. The National Park Service has restored most of the original buildings which now house park offices, the park library, and interns who teach at the Cuyahoga Valley Environmental Education Center.

At Hunt Farm the Valley Trail meets up with the Ohio & Erie Canal Towpath Trail, both using a steel and wood bridge to cross Furnace Run. A wayside here describes the former Furnace Run aqueduct. Just after the bridge, leave the Towpath Trail and head west through the woods to Riverview Road. Continue across Riverview Road, where you will come to the Valley Railway. Watch and listen for the train, then proceed cautiously over the crossing designed especially for horses. The trail meanders through the woods, between Furnace Run on the left and fields on your right. Glimpses of the Everett Road Covered Bridge and the Church in the Valley lend an old-time feel to your ride.

The Valley Trail ends at the Everett Road Covered Bridge Trailhead (where there is a small parking lot, port-a-john, and picnic table). Just across the bridge you reach the intersection with the Riding Run and Perkins Trails.

Riding Run Trail

Riding Run Trail starts at the Everett Road Covered Bridge, follows Oak Hill Road, then forms a loop trail in the forested area between Everett and Wheatley Roads. The trail has several steep climbs, bridges, and about 2 miles of wide, graveled path. In the spring, daffodils brighten the secluded meadows and you might see deer bounding ahead on the trail.

To reach Riding Run Trail, begin at the Everett Road Covered Bridge, on Everett Road one-half mile west of Riverview Road. For longer rides, you can begin at Langes Run Trail in the Wetmore Bridle Trail system, and use the Valley Trail to reach Riding Run (a round-trip length of 10 miles).

Starting from the west end of the covered bridge, go straight, following the trail as it goes alongside Oak Hill Road and Furnace Run. Make a right turn at Everett Road and use the stone equestrian trail alongside Everett Road. The trail bears right, towards Furnace Run, winding its way through a grove of white pines. The trail then takes a left turn to cross Everett Road and climbs a small slope. Here the loop trail begins. Our description follows the trail in a counterclockwise direction.

Having a wonderful time

To begin the loop, bear to the right and climb a short distance. The trail emerges onto a wide, graveled roadbed, formerly Meirs Road. This section of township road was abandoned in the 1950s, and the western end was officially .

abandoned in 1994. Follow this road uphill for .75 mile, passing a pine woods along the way. The reward upon reaching the top of the ridge is a secluded meadow filled with wildflowers and apple trees. Look closely for the remains of a chimney and other signs of the barn and two houses that once stood here.

The trail turns towards the south and continues on the old roadbed for another mile. This nearly level stretch of trail provides great vantage points for seeing down into the steeply cut Riding Run valley. Everett Road is visible as you reach the trail sign marking the halfway point. A clearing near here with exotic plantings marks another house site. The trail turns now and parallels Everett Road.

About a half mile further along, a trail to the right crosses Everett Road and connects the Riding Run loop to the Perkins loop on the south side of the road. Past the intersection, Riding Run continues straight ahead through a wooded area. Two bridges take you across streams before climbing back up to the top of the ridge, where the scent of pine sweetens the air. From this high spot you can glimpse the Cuyahoga River to the east.

Leaving the ridge, the trail descends a steep switchback and crosses a small stream before reconnecting to the start of the loop. Turning right, you soon reach Everett Road and can retrace your route to the covered bridge.

Riding Run
3.25 MILES
RIDING TIME – 1.5 HOURS
ELEVATION CHANGE – 260 FEET
RATING – MODERATE TO DIFFICULT

Perkins
3.75 MILES
RIDING TIME – 2 HOURS
ELEVATION CHANGE – 260 FEET
RATING – DIFFICULT

WHEATLY ROAD
FURNACE RUN
OAK HILL ROAD
EVERETT
EVERETT ROAD
EVERETT ROAD
EVERETT ROAD COVERED BRIDGE
VALLEY TRAIL
OAK HILL ROAD

Perkins Trail

The Perkins Trail is shaped like a narrow balloon at the end of a long string. It begins at the Everett Road Covered Bridge; about a mile from the start a connector trail links the Perkins Trail to the Riding Run Trail, across Everett Road. The steep hills and narrow paths of the Perkins Trail contribute to its "difficult" rating. Much of the trail also tends to be muddy. Nonetheless, it is worth the effort, as the trail takes you into some of the valley's more remote and quiet forests and stream ravines, areas beautifully typical of this northeast Ohio landscape.

This trail was named after Simon Perkins, the founder of Akron. Perkins was a friend of Canal Commissioner Alfred E. Kelley who convinced Perkins to donate land around and in Akron for canal development. This move resulted in the present route of the canal and assured the prosperous future of Akron. County maps for 1856 show that Simon Perkins owned land here as well, south of Everett Road.

To reach Perkins Trail, park at the Everett Road Covered Bridge Trailhead on Everett Road, one-half mile west of Riverview Road. For a longer ride, begin at Langes Run Trail in the Wetmore Bridle Trail system, and use the Valley Trail to reach Riding Run (a round-trip length of 10 miles).

Starting at the west end of the covered bridge, go a short ways alongside Oak Hill Road, then cross Oak Hill Road and go into a white pine woods. A severe storm in the summer of 1996 damaged many of the trees in this area. In a short distance the trail passes through an opening, and heads towards the wooded hillside. The climb up the hillside begins with switchbacks up the steepest section, then becomes more gradual. The entire ascent to the ridgetop is about 1 mile. Mature beeches and oaks border the trail; near the top you go into an old clearing that is now filling with hawthorns and other pioneer trees.

The trail picks up an old lane, and soon reaches the intersection where the loop part of the trail begins. Go straight to follow the trail clockwise. The trail swings to the south and follows a pretty beech ridge. Large shagbark hickories and oaks also surround the trail here in this high, open woods. The trail leaves the woods and comes into a clearing above Hale Farm and Village. For a short distance you are on Hale Farm property; an oil well is here in the center of a grassy meadow. On a clear day you can see across the Cuyahoga River valley to Cuyahoga Falls and beyond.

Go past the oil well, following a buried cable right-of-way, and watch for where the trail makes a sharp turn to the right. (This is the outermost point along the trail and it now turns to complete the loop.) Descend the steep trail into the creek valley, cross the creek, and begin a more moderate climb part way up the opposite hillside, then follow the trail down again to parallel the creek, a tributary flowing to Furnace Run. Watch for where the trail crosses back across the main creek to follow it along the opposite side. Just before crossing the creek the third time, you will reach a trail junction. The Perkins Trail turns abruptly to the right, leaving the valley, and climbs via a switchback to reach the top of the hill. The trail straight ahead at the junction connects Perkins Trail to Riding Run Trail by crossing the creek and following an old road up to Everett Road. The Riding Run Trail is just across the road and a short distance into the woods.

On the Perkins Trail, once you have reached the top of the hill, the trail continues on level ground a short distance until it reconnects to the point where the loop trail began. Turn to the left and retrace the beginning of your ride to return to the Everett Road Covered Bridge, a downhill trip of about 1 mile.

At work at Hale Farm

Hale Farm

The Hale Farm Trail is one of the new trails added since the first edition of the Trail Guide Handbook *and is one of the multi-use trails connecting to the Ohio & Erie Canal Towpath Trail. It connects the Towpath Trail to Hale Farm and Village. The section west of the railroad tracks was designed to be used by motorized trams carrying railroad passengers to and from Hale Farm, hence the wide, paved treadway. Much of the trail's alignment follows an AT&T transcontinental cable right-of-way. The Hale Farm Trail is a pleasant little trail which climbs through a scenic stretch of woods with the pastoral view of Hale Farm and Village as a reward.*

The trail can be reached from the Indigo Lake Trailhead which is on Riverview Road, about halfway between Bolanz and Ira Roads. The description begins at the parking lot.

Hale Farm
1 MILE
HIKING TIME – 30 MINUTES
BIKING TIME – 10 MINUTES
ELEVATION CHANGE – 120 FEET
RATING – EASY

WESTERN RESERVE VILLAGE
HALE FARM
OAK HILL ROAD
INDIGO LAKE
IRA CEMETERY
RIVERVIEW ROAD
CUYAHOGA RIVER
TOWPATH TRAIL

From the Indigo Lake parking lot, the trail east leads to the Towpath Trail. The trail to the west goes to Hale Farm and Village. Just across the tracks of the Cuyahoga Valley Scenic Railroad, Indigo Lake comes into view. Indigo Lake was created when a sand and gravel operation struck an underground aquifer. A local story says the operator of the bulldozer abandoned his machine and scrambled up the steep banks to safety. The bulldozer - so the story goes - is still down there! How much of the tale is true is anybody's guess, but there is no doubt that the lake is fed from more than just rainwater. The clarity of the water gives it the color for which it is named.

As you continue west, the tramway route circles around the north side of the lake and then gently climbs through a mature forest. Along the way are scattered "erratics" uncovered during construction and cast to the side. Erratics are boulders brought here by the glaciers from up north and consisting of a type of bedrock, such as granite, not normally found in northeast Ohio. Soon the trail reaches its pinnacle in an obviously planted stand of black walnut trees. Just as the trail heads down the final grade to Hale Farm there is a wonderful view of the pastoral setting in which Jonathan Hale chose to locate his home.

An entrance fee is charged. The Gatehouse which serves as a visitor center also serves food and includes a gift shop. See the Appendix for more information on Hale Farm and Village.

171

The O'Neil House

O'Neil Woods Metro Park

O'Neil Woods was acquired by Metro Parks, Serving Summit County, in 1969 when the family of the late William and Grace O'Neil leased their family farm to the park district, then later donated the farm outright, for public use and enjoyment. The O'Neil family had enjoyed the farm for two decades, using it for gentleman farming, horseback riding, and family outings.

A picnic grove is now located near the remains of their barn. Part of the foundation and an animal trough are still there, though overgrown. Picnic tables, grills, and toilets are all near the parking lot. A large old white pine stands sentinel over the "Lone Pine" area where you start and end Deer Run Trail. A section of the Buckeye Trail also uses part of Deer Run Trail.

Deer Run Trail

Deer Run Trail is located in O'Neil Woods, a unit of Metro Parks, Serving Summit County. You can reach O'Neil Woods Metro Park by taking Riverview Road to Ira Road. Turn west on Ira, then left onto Martin Road. The entrance to O'Neil Woods is less than a mile up Martin Road.

Deer Run Trail follows high ridges, drops down to Yellow Creek, then climbs back up a steep hillside to finish the 1.8 mile loop. Though relatively short, the climbs provide a good workout. Areas of mature upland oak forest, streamside sycamores and willows, fields of goldenrods, and an alder swamp are all found along this trail. The diversity of habitat makes it a favorite trail for birders.

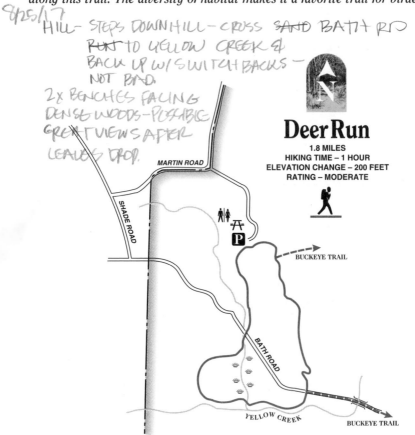

8/25/17
HILL- STEPS DOWNHILL - CROSS SAND BATH RD
RUN TO YELLOW CREEK &
BACK UP W/ SWITCHBACKS -
NOT BAD.
2X BENCHES FACING
DENSE WOODS - POSSIBLE
GREAT VIEWS AFTER
LEAVES DROP.

Deer Run
1.8 MILES
HIKING TIME – 1 HOUR
ELEVATION CHANGE – 200 FEET
RATING – MODERATE

MARTIN ROAD

SHADE ROAD

P

BUCKEYE TRAIL

BATH ROAD

YELLOW CREEK

BUCKEYE TRAIL

B egin Deer Run Trail at the eastern edge of the parking area, hiking the loop in a clockwise direction. Watch for the Metro Parks' deer print symbol sign which mark the trail. As you begin the loop, you pass through old fields which are managed for bluebird habitat. These fields are also favored habitat for wood cocks, or "timberdoodles," which perform their mating rituals here in early spring.Entering an oak woods, you will find a bench strategically placed at the trail summit overlooking a steep drop. As you descend the 70 steps along the ridge you can get some nice views off to the southeast. More steps and switch-backs take you to the valley below, a total descent of 180 feet. Large sugar maples mark the site where the O'Neil's old farmhouse once stood.

Cross Bath Road and follow the trail towards Yellow Creek, a major tributary which enters the Cuyahoga River about 1 mile further downstream. Here large sycamores, willows, cottonwoods, and black walnuts line the path along the stream. You can also find several varieties of ferns, many wildflowers, plus three kinds of vines—rope-like bittersweet, greenbrier, and virgin's bower. Several small bridges take the trail across side creeks. Leaving Yellow Creek, Deer Run Trail passes through a field and along an alder swamp, one of few in Summit County.

The trail crosses a creek on stepping stones, then again crosses Bath Road and begins the climb back to the picnic area. You will climb about 150 feet in one-third of a mile, edging a narrow ravine cut by the side creek. This gets your heart pumping! Again, benches along the way provide some welcome rest and views of the wooded ravine. The trail emerges from the woods at the top of the ridge into the picnic area near where you began.

The Old Bridge at Hampton Hills

Hampton Hills Metro Park

Hampton Hills Metro Park is within the boundaries of Cuyahoga Valley National Recreation Area but is owned and managed by Metro Parks, Serving Summit County. The rugged topography from the floor of the Cuyahoga Valley to the eastern ridge makes the hiking here moderate to difficult. You can also find a variety of habitats including streams, ravines, fields, and forests. This "park with all the bridges" is very popular with children because of the many log bridges spanning Adam Run and its side creeks.

The 278 acres of Hampton Hills were acquired in two main parcels. In 1964 the City of Akron leased 116 acres of wooded ravines along Akron Peninsula Road to the park district in exchange for land at Goodyear Heights Metropolitan Park where the city wished to erect a water tower. In 1967, Rhea H. and E. Reginald Adam donated to the park district 162 acres of ravines and their hilltop farm, including their century old farmhouse. The farm area is known as Top O' The World—for good reason, as you will see when you visit the area. There are two trails in Hampton Hills, Adam Run Trail and Spring Hollow Trail; Adam Run Trail is the newest, constructed by the Youth Conservation Corps in 1979. Both trails leave from the edge of the main parking lot.

Hampton Hills Metro Park is located on Akron Peninsula Road between Steels Corners Road and Bath Road. The main entrance and parking area are located on Akron Peninsula Road just north of the intersection with Bath Road. Another entrance, primarily used by visitors to the Top O' The World area, is located on Bath Road east of Akron Peninsula Road. A picnic area (with grills but no water) and toilets are located near the main parking lot. A soccer field and ballfield, off Steels Corners Road, can be used by obtaining a permit from Metro Parks, Serving Summit County.

Adam Run Trail 9/4/17 FOLLOWS ALONG CREEK-NOT SO MANY BRIDGES 3.2mi total HILLS & STEPS, NICE MEAD...

Adam Run and Spring Hollow Trails in Hampton Hills Metro Park both start out together. Adam Run Trail, marked by a stream symbol on sign posts along the way, follows Adam Run upstream, climbs steeply to the east rim of the Cuyahoga River valley, and descends back again to the valley floor.

Hampton Hills Metro Park is located on Akron Peninsula Road between Steels Corners Road and Bath Road. The main entrance and parking area are located on Akron Peninsula Road just north of the intersection with Bath Road. Find the entrance to both trails at the edge of the parking lot away from Akron Peninsula Road.

Bear to the left to begin the loop. When you start these two trails, you are following the old East River Road which was relocated and renamed Akron Peninsula Road in the late 1920s, and you cross a plain iron-railed bridge that was part of East River Road. Other remnants of this old road can be found up and down the valley between Bath Road and Peninsula.

During the first half mile or so, follow the Adam Run valley upstream, crossing the creek eight times on bridges. The creek valley is a good area for spring wildflowers and for an unusual looking plant with hollow, evergreen, grooved stems. This is scouring rush, in the genus of plants called Equisetum. Equisetums are in a category of plants that thrived and dominated plant life 180-500 million years ago. Only this genus survives today. The common name for this plant comes from the fact that the stems, containing silica, have been used for scouring and polishing. The rushes are often found along stream borders where their underground horizontal branching system can help anchor the soil along the banks.

After about a half mile, the two trails split. Bear left to stay on Adam Run Trail which follows the main course of the stream. Continue to climb the ravine; as it steepens, 100 steps built into the steep hillside makes your climb a little easier! A Civilian Conservation Corps style bench at the top is a good place to enjoy the views into the ravines full of black walnuts, elms, and sycamores. As you continue, the trail climbs at a gentler grade before passing through a white pine plantation planted by Girl Scouts in 1968.

After the pines, you come out into the open and crisscross fields and old fence rows. These fields and fence rows create an edge effect which is favored by birds and other wildlife. In the fall, goldenrods gild the fields with their arching,

178

golden branches. By now you have climbed near the top of the east ridge of the valley and can begin to enjoy the views to the west. Two additional benches are located on the trail; the second of these is near where a side trail enters from Top O' The World area. This side trail takes you to the former farm house which is maintained as an example of mid-1800s Western Reserve style of architecture. You can still see the farm pond, orchard, and fields which now feed a variety of wild, rather than domesticated, inhabitants.

After leaving this area, follow the trail through a young woods and across three more bridges. Right after the third bridge, Adam Run Trail rejoins Spring Hollow Trail. Together these trails wind their way back down to the valley below, first going through an area which is changing from field to forest through the process of succession. As you head back into the valley, sets of steps make the descent a little easier. You end this hike along a section of trail that again follows the old East River Road alignment, leading back to the parking lot.

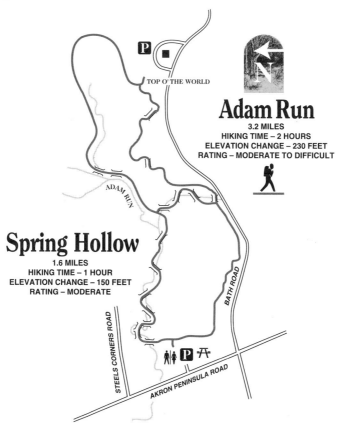

TOP O' THE WORLD

N

Adam Run

3.2 MILES
HIKING TIME – 2 HOURS
ELEVATION CHANGE – 230 FEET
RATING – MODERATE TO DIFFICULT

ADAM RUN

Spring Hollow

1.6 MILES
HIKING TIME – 1 HOUR
ELEVATION CHANGE – 150 FEET
RATING – MODERATE

BATH ROAD

STEELS CORNERS ROAD

AKRON PENINSULA ROAD

Spring Hollow Trail

9/4/17 *3.2 miles combined Adam & Spring*

Spring Hollow Trail in Hampton Hills Metro Park starts out along with Adam Run Trail, both following the route of the former East River Road. This road was relocated and is now Akron Peninsula Road. Trail signs with an oak leaf symbol mark the Spring Hollow Trail. It makes a shorter loop than the much longer Adam Run Trail, going just part way up Adam Run, but still includes a strenuous climb up a side creek.

Hampton Hills Metro Park is located on Akron Peninsula Road between Steels Corners Road and Bath Road. The main entrance and parking area are located on Akron Peninsula Road just north of the intersection with Bath Road.

From the parking lot, bear left (north) to begin the trail in a clockwise direction. Soon the trail bears to the right and winds its way up the Adam Run valley, crossing and recrossing the creek eight times. In just over a half mile, the two trails split; for Spring Hollow go straight ahead, continuing along a side creek.

You now head up a deep, picturesque ravine. There are many fallen trees along the steep banks, with several straddling the narrow stream bed. Boardwalks and log bridges makes the going easier over the stream soaked base of the ravine. The last gasp climb to the top of the ravine has a total of 75 steps and rises more than 50 feet. A bench at the top provides a welcome resting place.

At the top of the hill, rejoin Adam Run Trail which enters from the left. The two trails, now joined, cross a scrub meadow area. The meadow still has berry bushes, but is slowly but surely becoming forest once again. Just after entering the woods, begin the descent back down into the valley; two sets of steps makes the going a little easier. You can find plenty of large oaks up on the drier upland sections of this trail, and walnuts, slippery elms, maples, and sycamores in the wetter ravines. In places, wild grape vines have created openings in the forest canopy where you might find birds feasting on the grapes. The last stretch of this trail is on the old East River Road alignment; it then ends at the parking lot where you began.

About the Editors

Rob Bobel oversaw production of the second edition and was primarily responsible for graphics and layout. He is a civil engineer in the Technical Assistance and Professional Services Division of Cuyahoga Valley National Recreation Area and serves on the board of the Ohio & Erie Canal Corridor Coalition and the Ohio to Erie Trail Fund. He was charter trail boss for the Cuyahoga Valley Trails Council and serves as chair of the publications committee.

Peg Bobel edited the second edition, revising nearly all the text. She is the Executive Director of the Cuyahoga Valley Association, a non-profit friends-of-the-park group supporting the mission and programs of Cuyahoga Valley National Recreation Area. She was charter president of the Cuyahoga Valley Trails Council and, along with her husband, was one of the founding members of the group.

About the Book

Trail Guide Handbook was designed and typeset on a Macintosh in Quark XPress® by Jef Sturm Graphic Design, Akron, Ohio. The book is set in Clearface. The maps were drawn in Adobe Illustrator 6.0 from 7.5 minute scale line overlays taken from USGS quad sheets. The layout of some of the newer trails was mapped in the field using a Trimble Pathfinder global positioning system (GPS) unit.

The book was printed by Franklin Printing Company on sixty pound Eastern Opaque Polar White paper containing 50% recycled fibers (minimum 20% post consumer waste).

Appendix

General Information

For more information on park areas and facilities referred to in this guide, write or call:

Superintendent
Cuyahoga Valley National
Recreation Area
15610 Vaughn Road
Brecksville, OH 44141
216-526-5256

Canal Visitor Center
216-524-1497

Happy Days Visitor Center
216-650-4636

Cleveland Metroparks
4101 Fulton Parkway
Cleveland, OH 44144
216-351-6300

Brecksville Nature Center
216-526-1012

Metro Parks, Serving Summit County
975 Treaty Line Road
Akron, OH 44313-5898
330-867-5511

Seiberling Naturealm
330-865-8065
330-836-2185

For information on the National Park System, access ParkNet at
http://www.nps.gov

Reservable Picnic Shelters

Following is a list of reservable picnic areas. A fee is charged for use of these areas, including use of a covered picnic shelter or enclosed pavilion with meeting space. Each reservable shelter is surrounded by a large outdoor play area and access to hiking trails. All have cooking grills and restrooms.

Cleveland Metroparks (216-351-6300)

> Brecksville Reservation:
> Ottawa Point
>
> Bedford Reservation:
> Lost Meadows (reservable on weekends only)
>
> Reservations are taken starting January 2 for the current year.

Metro Parks, Serving Summit County (330-867-5511)

> Furnace Run:
> Brushwood Pavilion   (reservable six months in advance; enclosed and includes kitchen with refrigerator and coffee maker and wood burning fireplace)

Cuyahoga Valley National Recreation Area (216-524-2248)

> Ledges Shelter
> Octagon Shelter
>
> Reservations are open on January 2 and must be made at least four weeks in advance. Fee is half price for persons with Golden Age Passports or Golden Access cards.

Organizations

Cuyahoga Valley Trails Council is an all-volunteer group dedicated to building and maintaining trails in the Cuyahoga Valley. In addition to trail guide publications such as the *Trail Guide Handbook*, the group conducts monthly trail work sessions throughout the Cuyahoga Valley. For more information write:

Cuyahoga Valley Trails Council
1607 Delia Avenue
Akron, OH 44320

Buckeye Trail Association, Inc., which maintains the BT, is an all-volunteer group organized and operated exclusively to construct, maintain, and encourage use of the Buckeye Trail. For membership information and guides to the Buckeye Trail in other parts of Ohio, write:

Buckeye Trail Association, Inc.
P.O. Box 254
Worthington, OH, 43085.

Cuyahoga Valley Association is CVNRA's non-profit friends group dedicated to assisting the recreation area through fundraising and supporting its programs. For membership information write or call:

Cuyahoga Valley Association
P.O. Box 222
Peninsula, OH 44264
216-657-2909

Cuyahoga Valley Environmental Education Center, operated by the Cuyahoga Valley Association and the National Park Service, has a weekday residential environmental education program for grades 4-7 and has special weekend and summer programs for adults and families. For information write or call:

Cuyahoga Valley Environmental Education Center
3675 Oak Hill Road
Peninsula, OH 44264
216-657-2796

Ohio and Erie Canal Association is a non-profit membership group working to develop the Ohio & Erie Canal National Heritage Corridor from Cleveland to Zoar. For information write or call:

Ohio and Erie Canal Association
520 South Main Street
Suite 2541-F
Akron, OH 44311
330-434-5657

Overnight Lodging

The Inn at Brandywine Falls
George and Katie Hoy, Innkeepers
8230 Brandywine Road
Sagamore Hills, OH 44067
216-467-1812 or 216-650-4965
Call for reservations

Hosteling International's
Stanford House AYH Hostel
6093 Stanford Road
Peninsula, OH 44264
216-467-8711
Reservations advised for weekends; any age welcome;
not necessary to be AYH member

Other Attractions

Cuyahoga Valley Scenic Railroad
P.O. Box 158
1630 West Mill Street
Peninsula, OH 44264-0158
800-468-4070
216-657-2000

Hale Farm and Village
2686 Oak Hill Road
Bath, OH 44210-0296
330-666-3711

Boston Mills/Brandywine Ski Resorts
216-655-6703
216-467-2242

Dover Lake Waterpark
216-467-SWIM

Maps

For maps and travel information:

4 Corners Map Shop
1887 West Market Street
Akron, OH 44313
330-869-6277

The Trails

TRAIL	HIKE	SKI	BIKE	HORSE	LENGTH	ELEVATION	DIFFICULTY
Adam Run	🚶				3.20	230	✓✓✓
All Purpose - Bedford	🚶	🎿	🚲		5.25	120	✓✓
All Purpose - Brecksville	🚶	🎿	🚲		4.50	410	✓✓
Bike & Hike	🚶		🚲		10.1	min	✓
Blue Hen Falls	🚶				1.20	110	✓
Boston Run	🚶	🎿			3.40	80	✓✓
Brandywine Gorge	🚶				1.25	160	✓✓
Bridal Veil Falls	🚶				0.25	30	✓
Bridle Trail - Bedford				🐎	6.00	270	✓✓✓
Bridle Trail - Brecksville				🐎	9.00	260	✓✓✓
Bridle Trail - Pinery Narrows				🐎	3.00	8	✓
Buckeye Trail							
Egbert to Frazee	🚶				7.60	290	✓✓✓
Frazee to Station Rd	🚶				2.50	8	✓
Station Rd to Red Lock	🚶				7.00	200	✓✓✓
Red Lock to Boston	🚶				5.60	250	✓✓✓
Boston to Pine Lane	🚶				4.00	240	✓✓
Pine Lane to Everett	🚶				4.10	150	✓
Everett to Bath Rd	🚶				3.00	160	✓✓
Butler				🐎	0.75	150	✓
Buttonwood	🚶	🎿			1.00	min	✓
Chippewa Creek	🚶				2.50	220	✓✓
Cross Country	🚶	🎿			2.50	160	✓✓
Deer Lick Cave	🚶				4.00	205	✓✓✓
Deer Run	🚶				1.80	200	✓✓
Dickerson Run				🐎	1.00	175	✓
Forest Point	🚶				0.50	min	✓
H.S. Wagner Daffodil	🚶	🎿			1.00	min	✓
Hale Farm	🚶		🚲		1.00	120	✓
Haskell Run	🚶				0.50	70	✓
Hemlock Creek Loop	🚶	🎿			0.60	min	✓

TRAIL	HIKE	SKI	BIKE	HORSE	LENGTH	ELEVATION	DIFFICULTY
Lake	🚶				1.00	min	✔
Langes Run				🏇	4.50	190	✔✔✔
Ledges	🚶				2.20	105	✔✔
My Mountain	🚶				1.50	100	✔
Oak Hill	🚶	⛷			1.50	50	✔
Ohio & Erie Canal Towpath							
Lock 39 to Frazee	🚶	⛷	🚴		3.75	20	✔
Frazee to Station Rd	🚶	⛷	🚴		2.50	8	✔
Station Rd to Red Lock	🚶	⛷	🚴		2.50	20	✔
Red Lock to Boston Store	🚶	⛷	🚴		1.75	15	✔
Boston Store to Lock 29	🚶	⛷	🚴		2.50	30	✔
Lock 29 to Hunt Farm	🚶	⛷	🚴		3.00	25	✔
Hunt Farm to Ira Rd	🚶	⛷	🚴		1.75	6	✔
Ira Rd to Indian Mound	🚶	⛷	🚴		1.75	25	✔
Old Carriage	🚶	⛷			3.25	180	✔✔✔
Old Mill	🚶				1.00	min	✔
Perkins				🏇	3.75	260	✔✔✔✔
Pine Grove	🚶				2.20	100	✔✔
Plateau	🚶	⛷			4.50	200	✔✔✔
Quarry	🚶				1.20	120	✔
Riding Run				🏇	3.25	260	✔✔✔
Rock Creek	🚶	⛷			1.20	min	✔
Salt Run	🚶				3.25	160	✔✔✔
Scenic Overlook	🚶				0.25	20	✔
Spring Hollow	🚶				1.60	150	✔✔
Stanford	🚶				1.50	190	✔✔
Tabletop				🏇	0.75	100	✔
Towpath	🚶				1.30	120	✔
Tree Farm	🚶	⛷			2.75	80	✔
Valley				🏇	2.75	40	✔
Valley Stream	🚶				0.50	50	✔
Wetmore				🏇	4.00	250	✔✔

Index

Page numbers in italics refer to maps.

Trail Notes